£2.99

A Taste of the
GOOD LIFE

A Taste of the
GOOD LIFE

RICHARD & ANN BRIERS

PAVILION

To Annie's Mum, who is so devoted to cooking that it is
often hard to get her out of the kitchen!
To my Aunt Sheila, who produces delicious dishes
on a low budget and
To Michèle Brown, who helped us put it all together
This book is dedicated.

First published in Great Britain in 1995 by
Pavilion Books Limited
26 Upper Ground
London SE1 9PD

Anthology copyright © 1995 by Complete Editions Ltd
For individual text copyrights see page 223
All black and white illustrations copyright © Mary Evans Picture Library
Jacket photograph by Neil Setchfield

The moral right of the editors has been asserted

Designed by Nigel Partridge

A CIP catalogue record for this book is available from the British Library

ISBN 1-85793-583 7

Typeset in Stempel Garamond
Printed and bound in Great Britain by Hartnolls

2 4 6 8 10 9 7 5 3 1

This book may be ordered by post direct from the publisher.
Please contact the Marketing Department.
But try your bookshop first.

CONTENTS

Go thy way, eat thy bread with joy, and drink thy wine
with a merry heart.
ECCLESIASTES 9:7

Dost thou think, because thou art virtuous, there shall be no
more cakes and ale?
WILLIAM SHAKESPEARE, *TWELFTH NIGHT (ACT 2, SCENE3)*, 1600–1601

PREFACE

When we first talked of compiling an anthology about the pleasures of the table and the good things of life generally, we felt it really wouldn't be complete without a reference to friends. A delicious meal or a relaxing drink are even more pleasurable when enjoyed in congenial company. The French cookery writer Edouard de Pomiane sums it up perfectly in this description of a simple lunch he cooked for a group of close friends in his tiny cottage in the country:

And now there is a succession of joys:
The eggs with a glass of cider – just like velvet.
The roast with its gravy, and the mushrooms that I warmed whilst I was dishing up the roast – a rustic cooking with a primitive freshness. With this, a glass of Burgundy.
The peas follow, soothingly bland.
The cheese... The strawberries and cream... The coffee... A thimbleful of plum brandy...
Contentment... The joy of living and of loving one's friends.

So this collection owes much to our friends, their conversation and stories as well as their recipes and hospitality.

Having established the feel of the book we cast around for a title that said it all. We can't remember which of us came up with the final version but each has congratulated the other on their brilliance, so honour is satisfied. A Taste of the Good Life! What a lot of happy memories that phrase conjures up for us. As well as thoughts of food, wine and good company it reminds us of the television series *The Good Life*. Incredibly the programme is now twenty years old. It was about being self-sufficient in the suburbs: growing your own food, raising your own livestock, inventing ingenious devices to take the place of the twentieth century's energy-guzzling machines. Most of all it was about being independent and self-reliant. The idea struck a chord with millions of people tied down by the burden of earning their daily crust and placating the boss.

It embodied a truth we have discovered ourselves over the years: that, like everything worth while, the good life largely depends on your own efforts. And it's all the better when you have something to compare it with. When we started out on married life, as two struggling actors in the late 1950s, we were pretty broke and home was a bed-sit. No fine wines or exotic dishes for us. Our main aim was to fill ourselves up as much as possible for as little money as possible. Yet even this had its charms. When Pooter, the endearing hero of *The Diary of a Nobody*, confided in the pages of his journal, 'I could not help thinking that half the pleasures of life were derived from the little struggles and small privations that one had to endure at the beginning of one's married life,' he could well have been describing us.

We first met while working in rep. at the Liverpool Playhouse and it wasn't long before we became what is known these days as 'an item' – Richard and Annie. As with most romances, food was part of our courtship ritual. Annie still vividly remembers the first meal cooked for her by her future husband. The menu was made up of the following delights: soup from a packet (Florida Spring Vegetable, to be strictly accurate), baked beans on toast and tinned fruit salad, all washed down with a cup of tea. Our recollection is that it all tasted wonderful because the company was so good and because the food was so beautifully presented, with the toast for the baked beans cut up into neat little triangles! It's certainly true that since then we have always enjoyed eating together, even the simplest meal, and we both agree that good company enhances the pleasure of any meal, even one as humble as that youthful offering.

One of our early extravagances was a rather quaint device called a Dutch oven, which we purchased for the princely sum of 19s 6d (97½p), from Barkers department store in Kensington High Street. This was like a large, square biscuit tin with little legs. It could be placed over the single gas-ring, which was all we had to cook on, and functioned as something approximating to a real oven. One of the small triumphs regularly achieved under these challenging conditions was a version of shepherd's pie, made with just a hint of meat and a lot of vegetables, topped with mounds of mashed potato. Annie's mother, a perfectly splendid cook who loves cooking for others, had devised this dish during the war to make one ration of meat go round twelve hungry fire-fighters, so it suited two broke young actors with healthy appetites extremely well.

But of course as we've grown older, and our bank balance has improved, we've had the good fortune to experience a far wider range of culinary delights than we ever dreamed of in those far-off bed-sit days. We've improved on our cooking skills and become more adventurous in our tastes. We've been fortunate enough to eat at some superb restaurants and in the houses of friends who are great cooks and knowledgeable wine buffs. We've tasted, sipped, read, cooked and laughed our way through nearly forty years together. This book is a reflection of our own personal tastes summed up in the words of some of the world's best writers and chefs. We hope it gives a flavour of all the pleasures the kitchen and cellar have to offer, from the humblest home-made loaf to 'the Chopin among wines' – champagne. Most of all we hope it is a collection to tickle the palate of everyone who appreciates 'a taste of the good life'.

ANN AND RICHARD BRIERS

BARBECUES

M y first attempt at barbecuing was, of course, a total disaster, as many first attempts are. I didn't allow enough time for the briquettes to heat up and turn white. The rain began to fall as the light faded and I finally finished cooking with the aid of a torch and an umbrella. Annie and our guests had long since retired into the house, and most of them were too tight to enjoy the food when at last it arrived. Not to put too fine a point on it – it was a fiasco.

My old friend, that splendid actor John Thaw, also had his ups and downs before achieving success. I remember the fateful evening when he was cooking for us at his home and discovered he had run out of ignition fuel. He substituted paraffin, which is not only highly dangerous but also resulted in the most appalling sausages I've ever tasted! Since then he and I have followed the advice of that Master Barbie Chef, the television and film producer Alvin Rakoff: four fire-lighters tucked under the charcoal and success is guaranteed every time.

Another hot (ouch!) barbecue tip comes from Ernie Wise, who, like me, is interested in cost-cutting. If you cannot afford an elaborate barbecue he suggests building some ordinary house bricks into an oven shape and bunging a metal foot-scraper across the top but it works brilliantly.

I had my first experience of outdoor cooking many years before Richard and I bought a barbecue. As teenagers, my sister Sally and I used to go camping for a week every summer, initially with the Girl Guides and later with the Sea Rangers. These camps were supervised – marvellously – by Eileen Scott, who was called Skipper, and I know it wasn't *her* fault that the food tent collapsed completely one year during a gale-lashed week in North Wales.

Skipper taught us to cut and roll back the grass to each side of the rectangle where we lit our cooking fire. That way, at the end of the week, when the last fire was completely cold, we could roll the grass back and the field would look as it had done before we arrived. For me there is something about the nostalgic aroma of woodsmoke that beats the smell of a 'barbie' fire any day. But as Richard is not generally one for the great outdoors I am pleased that he does enjoy barbecuing and I leave the cooking to him. Here is a recipe in which all *my* work is done beforehand.

Barbecued Chicken in a Spicy Marinade

Make a marinade by combining the following ingredients and mixing well:

3 tablespoons groundnut or vegetable oil
1 tablespoon sesame oil, if possible (if not available use olive oil)
2 tablespoons soy sauce
1 tablespoon lemon juice
1 teaspoon finely grated fresh ginger or ½ teaspoon ground ginger
1 garlic clove, crushed
1 fresh green chilli, finely chopped, or put the whole chilli into the marinade
and remove before cooking (optional)

12

2 teaspoons ground coriander
1 teaspoon brown sugar or clear honey
salt and freshly ground black pepper to taste
a little lemongrass, snipped small, gives an interesting additional flavour

Prepare either 10–12 chicken drumsticks or 8 boned, skinned chicken breasts as follows:

If using drumsticks, coat them with the marinade then leave them resting in any remaining marinade. If using chicken breasts, cut them into bite-size pieces to fit on a skewer then soak in the marinade, making sure all the pieces are well coated. Leave the chicken in the fridge for several hours or overnight.

Remove from the fridge an hour before cooking.

If using drumsticks, brush them again with the marinade, place on the preheated barbecue grill and cook until tender, basting occasionally with any remaining marinade or with a little additional oil. If using the cubed chicken breasts, thread them on to skewers, alternating with bite-size vegetable pieces such as onion quarters, mushrooms, chunks of courgette or red/green pepper. Brush the vegetables with a little oil, place the skewers on the grill and watch carefully, basting from time to time with marinade or oil. It is a good idea if someone watches the cook watching the barbecue and keeps up his or her spirits with a generous glass of wine and lots of praise.

Serve the barbecued food acompanied by baked potatoes and garlic bread (easier if done in your kitchen oven) and a variety of salads.

BEER

Shakespeare and Bass are names known to every Briton, but one might suspect that most could speak with more authority about the latter.

EDWARD AND LORNA BUNYARD, *THE EPICURE'S COMPANION*, 1937

I was first introduced to draught Bass and its beatific side effects in my teens, during my time as an office boy. To my mind beer has *not* improved in the ensuing years. The advent of ice-cold lager was regrettable in my opinion. It is hardly suitable to the British climate and comes as a shock to the stomach. Beer should be a comforting drink, served from the wood at around blood heat, with the minimum amount of gas. That way the first half of a desperately needed pint can be quaffed in one go, with no effort.

If, as I do, you prefer a quiet drink with a few friends at home, brewing your own is an option (though I don't recommend a recipe I came across for mangel-wurzel beer). The great danger of creating your own pub is that there is no one around to call 'last orders'. This can lead to domestic strife for the indulgent and weak-willed, which is why I don't have a still of my own in the house!

John Taylor's paean of praise for the virtues of ale is as true today as it was nearly four hundred years ago. What a comfort to know that at least some of the pleasures of a bygone age are still available to us today.

Ale is rightly called nappy, for it will set a nap upon a man's threadbare eyes when he is sleepy. It is called merry-goe-downe, for it slides down merrily. It is fragrant to the scent; it is most pleasant to taste; the flowing and mantling of it (like chequer work), with the verdant smile of it, is delightful to the sight; it is touching or feeling to the brain or heart;

and to please the senses all, it provokes men to singing and mirth, which is contenting to the hearing. The speedy taking of it dothe comfort the heavy and troubled minde; it will make a weeping widow laugh and forget sorrow for her deceased husband; it is truly termed the spirit of the buttery, for it puts spirit into all it enters. It makes the footman's head and heeles so light that he seems to fly as he runnes; it is the warmest lining of a naked man's coat; it satiates and assuages hunger and cold; with a toaste it is the poor man's comfort; the shepheard, mower, plowman, and blacksmith's jewell, the beggar's joy, and the prisoner's loving nurse; it will whet the wit so sharp that it will make a carter talk of things beyond his reach; it will set a bashful suitor a wooing; it heats the chill blood of the aged; it will cause a man to speak past his owne or any other man's capacity of understanding… it will put courage into a coward and make him swagger and fight; it is a seale to many a goode bargaine; the physician will commend it; the lawyer will defend it; it neither hurts nor kills any but those who abuse it unmeasurably and beyond bearing; it doth good to as many as take it rightly; it is as good as a paire of spectacles to clear the eyesight of an old parish clarke; and, in conclusion, it is such a nourisher of mankinde, that if my mouth were as bigge as Bishopsgate, my pen as long as a may-pole, and my inke a flowing spring or a standing fishpond, yet I could not, with mouth, pen, or inke, speake or write the true worthiness of ale.

JOHN TAYLOR, *THE BLESSINGS OF ALE*, 1580–1653

15

At a dinner-party in Paris, given by a French nobleman, I saw a black bottle of English porter set on the table as a great rarity, and drunk out of small glasses.

SAMUEL ROGERS, TABLE-TALK, 1856

BEER

O Beer! O Hodgson, Guinness, Allsopp, Bass!
Names that should be on every infant's tongue!
Shall days and months and years and centuries pass,
And still your merits be unrecked, unsung?
Oh,! I have gazed into my foaming glass,
And wished that lyre could yet again be strung
Which once rang prophet-like through Greece, and taught her
Misguided sons that the best drink was water...

CHARLES STUART CALVERLEY, 1872

St George he was for England,
And before he killed the dragon
He drank a pint of English Ale
Out of an English flagon.

G. K. CHESTERTON, *THE ENGLISHMAN*, 1900

These remarks are for beginners only, as there is no disagreement among experienced beer-drinkers that the tankard is the right thing to drink beer from, and that its smallest size is the pint. Learners in their toddling stages may be allowed to experiment with glasses holding half a pint till they gain confidence.

The tankard's great advantage, of course, is that it has a strong handle and is thus easier to raise than a pint glass would be. It has also considerable advantages in being able to lend emphasis to argument when returned to the table. No better full stop to a dogmatic statement has yet been elaborated.

EDWARD AND LORNA BUNYARD, *THE EPICURE'S COMPANION*, 1937

BOOKS

L ife without books would not be a good life as far as we are concerned. Annie and I are both keen readers, although our tastes differ. Annie collects old cookery books and tends to read them as though they were novels. I like to collect old books on what used to be called 'nature study' when I was a boy at school. I covet them for the beautiful bindings and illustrations as much as for their contents. Annie loves to get stuck into a challenging modern novel while I prefer theatrical biographies. On my forays into secondhand bookshops in search of natural history books I am easily distracted by autobiographies of great actors of the past – Irving, Ellen Terry, Forbes Robertson et al.

Harold Macmillan used to describe the ideal way of relaxing at the end of the day as going to bed with a good Trollope! However, when I'm away working, on a stage tour or film location, I find there's nothing so soothing after a hard day as a Big Dickens. What a writer that man was: so prolific and with almost as much insight into the oddities of human nature as Shakespeare himself. All the problems of the day are soon forgotten once you dip into the totally absorbing world of *Martin Chuzzlewit* or *Dombey and Son*. As another great man, Samuel Johnson, so wisely said two hundred years ago:

Keep yourself cheerful. Lie in bed with a lamp and when you cannot sleep and are beginning to think, light your candle and read.

No furniture so charming as books, even if you never open them or read a single word.

SYDNEY SMITH, 1771–1845

I sometimes wish for a catalogue of lounging books – books that one takes up in the gout, low spirits, *ennui*, or when one is waiting for company. Some novels, gay poetry, odd whimsical authors, as Rabelais etc., etc. A *catalogue raisonné* of such might itself be a good lounging book. I cannot read mere catalogues of books: they give me no ideas.

HORACE WALPOLE IN *THE LOUNGER'S COMMONPLACE BOOK*, 1805

W hen I was a young boy I adored the stories of P. G. Wodehouse. I must have read them all, many of them during a time when I occasionally played truant from school in order to spend the day sitting on Raynes Park Station platform engrossed in the world of that smoothie of a butler Jeeves, and his amiable ass of an employer, Bertie Wooster. So of course it was sheer delight when, some thirty years later, I was cast to play Wooster himself, opposite Michael Hordern as the urbane Jeeves, in the radio series *Oh Jeeves!* based on the Wodehouse stories. As a devoted fan I couldn't resist including a little of my hero in a collection of all that makes up the best in life.

Whatever Sir Watkyn Bassett's moral shortcomings he did his guests extraordinarily well at the festive board, and even in my preoccupied condition it was plain to me in the first five minutes that his cook was a woman who had the divine fire in her. From a Grade A soup we proceeded to a toothsome fish, and from the toothsome fish to a salmi of game which even Anatole might have been proud to sponsor. Add asparagus, a jam omelette, and some spirited sardines on toast, and you will see what I mean.

All wasted on me, of course. As the fellow said, better a dinner of herbs when you're all buddies together than a regular blow-out when you're not, and the sight of Gussie and Madeline Bassett sitting side by side at the other end of the table turned the food to ashes in my mouth.

You know what engaged couples are like in mixed company as a rule. They put their heads together and converse in whispers. They slap and giggle. They pat and prod. I have even known the female member of the duo to feed her companion with a fork. There was none of this sort of thing about Madeline Bassett and Gussie. He looked pale and corpse-like, she cold and proud and aloof. They put in the time for the most part making bread pills and, as far as I was able to ascertain, didn't exchange a word from start to finish. Oh, yes, once – when he asked her to pass the salt, and she passed the pepper, and he said 'I meant the salt,' and she said 'Oh really?' and passed the mustard.

P. G. WODEHOUSE, *THE CODE OF THE WOOSTERS*, 1938

———

Better is a dinner of herbs where love is, than a stalled ox and hatred therewith.

PROVERBS 15:17

BRANDY

Claret is the liquor for boys; port for men; but he who aspires to be a hero must drink brandy... brandy will do soonest for a man what drinking *can* do for him.

DR JOHNSON IN JAMES BOSWELL, *LIFE OF SAMUEL JOHNSON*, 1791

Brandy, and indeed all other drams, should be taken at one sup, no matter how large the glass may be. The old rule of 'never to take two bites of the cherry', applies with peculiar emphasis to cherry brandy.

WILLIAM MAGINN, *MAXIMS OF SIR WILLIAM O'DOHERTY, BART.*, 1849

Thursday, New Year's Eve 1874
Edwin Law told me of an infallible receipt for warming cold and wet feet on a journey. Pour half a glass of brandy into each boot.

FRANCIS KILVERT, *DIARY 1870–79*

It is to the benefit of our livers and our bank balance that Richard and I are not able to drink brandy without waking halfway through the night with our hearts racing away and our minds wide awake. However, we do love to use brandy in cooking: a small amount adds zest to the simplest dish and we take comfort from the assurance that cooking really does take out the alcohol and leave just the unique flavour. We do *not* recommend using the sort of liquid gold described in the following extract as a mere cooking brandy. Heads have rolled in France for less!

The cognac was not to Rex's taste. It was clear and pale and it came to

21

us in a bottle free from grime and Napoleonic cyphers. It was only a
year or two older than Rex and lately bottled. They gave it to us in very
thin tulip-shaped glasses of modest size.

'Brandy's one of the things I do know a bit about,' said Rex. 'This is
a bad colour. What's more, I can't taste it in this thimble.'

They brought him a balloon the size of his head. He made them warm
it over the spirit lamp. Then he rolled the splendid spirit round, buried
his face in the fumes, and pronounced it the sort of stuff he put soda in
at home.

So, shamefacedly, they wheeled out of its hiding place the vast and
mouldy bottle they kept for people of Rex's sort.

'That's the stuff,' he said, tilting the treacly concoction till it left dark
rings round the sides of his glass. 'They've always got some tucked away,
but they won't bring it out unless you make a fuss. Have some.'

'I'm quite happy with this.'

'Well, it's a crime to drink it, if you don't really appreciate it.'

He lit his cigar and sat back at peace with the world; I, too, was at
peace in another world than his. We both were happy.

EVELYN WAUGH, BRIDESHEAD REVISITED, 1945

BREAD

13 July 1665
... and so I went by water, at night late, to Sir G. Carterets. But there
being no oares to carry me, I was fain to call a Sculler that had a gentleman already in it; and he proved a man of love to Musique and he
and I sung together the way down – with great pleasure, and an accident extraordinary to be met with. There came to Dinner, they having
dined, but my Lady caused something to be brought for me and I dined
well, and mighty merry, especially my Lady Slany and I about eating
of Creame and brown bread – which she loves as much as I.

SAMUEL PEPYS' *DIARY*

I am not quite sure if Samuel Pepys and his friend took jam with their
bread and cream so that it was rather like scones, or whether it was
just a richer version of the simple bread and milk once so popular in
British nurseries. Either way it was clearly a good comfort food. In our
house, when we are feeling rather low and want a bit of comfort we
have found that a nice soothing bread and butter pudding fits the bill
perfectly.

BREAD AND BUTTER PUDDING TO CHASE AWAY
THE BLUES
(unless, of course, it is your weight that is making you feel blue!)
These quantities serve 4.

6 thin slices white bread (with crusts removed), generously buttered
3 oz (75 g) mixed dried fruit to suit your taste
2 eggs
scant 1 oz (25 g) caster sugar

¾ pint (425 ml) full cream milk
2 tablespoons demerara sugar
grated nutmeg

Butter a 2-pint (1-litre) ovenproof dish. Cut the bread into triangles and place in the dish, layered with the dried fruit. Beat the eggs and caster sugar together with a little of the milk. Heat the remaining milk until hot but not boiling. Pour the hot milk on to the egg mixture, stirring as you pour, then gently pour this custard over the bread and fruit and leave to stand for approximately 1 hour. Sprinkle the surface with the demerara sugar and a dusting of grated nutmeg.

Stand the dish in a roasting pan and add enough hot water (not boiling) to come halfway up the sides of the dish. Bake at 150° C (300° F) gas mark 2 for 45–60 minutes, until the custard is set and the top of the pudding is golden and crispy.

Eat hot from the oven and feel your sense of well-being return – a process that is speeded up if a small dash of brandy is added to the custard before it is poured on to the bread and butter.

Devonshire is celebrated for the excellence of its bread, in Suffolk almost every cottager wife knows how to make it well, and in the North where large dairy farms are numerous. But in Kent, Sussex, Surrey, Middlesex, and many other parts of the Kingdom, not one woman in twenty is capable of making a loaf.

ELIZA ACTON, *THE ENGLISH BREAD-BOOK*, 1857

When at home, she [Emily] took the principal part of the cooking on herself, and did all the household ironing; and

24

after Tubby grew old and infirm, it was Emily who made all the bread for the family; and anyone passing by the kitchen door, might have seen her studying German out of an open book, propped up before her, as she kneaded the dough; but no study, however interesting, interfered with the goodness of the bread, which was always light and excellent.

MRS GASKELL, *THE LIFE OF CHARLOTTE BRONTË*, 1857

BREAKFAST

The cheapest breakfast I ever enjoyed was with Jon Akass, a great friend (alas no longer with us) who became a famous newspaper columnist. We were both eighteen years old and suffering the boredom of National Service: two downtrodden Air Force clerks, he burning to be a writer, I determined to be a great actor.

Because we were serving – albeit somewhat unwillingly – in Her Majesty's Forces, we were each allowed a free railpass once a year to go anywhere in Britain. We elected to take a free ride to Scotland. We arrived eventually at Inverness station, hung over and absolutely famished, having laughed all the way, helped along by a good deal of ghastly cheap vino.

Outside the station was a classic workman's caff, where we devoured the full Scots breakfast: a huge plate of porridge with salt (a new experience for Sassenachs), then three rashers of bacon, two fried eggs, two sausages, black pudding, fried bread (ah! fried bread) plus two doorsteps of white bread with a large pot of marmalade, accompanied by a quart of sweet tea. The bill for both of us was five shillings – 25p to you!

Porridge, as everyone knows, is one of the healthiest foods you can eat. We usually stick to cereals and bran in the morning when we are working because it's quicker, but when we are on holiday we have more time to enjoy the first meal of the day. The most exciting porridge I've ever tasted was served, funnily enough, not in our beloved Scotland but in a family-run hotel in the Lake District. When I ordered I was asked what I would like on it. Memories of Inverness prompted me to choose salt. There was a pause, then our host suggested I should try it with whisky. My eyes glittered and, avoiding Annie's raised eybrows, I said I would give it a try. I can assure you it's the best start to the day I've ever had. Only to be taken on holiday, of course.

26

By eating a hearty breakfast, you escape the temptation of luncheon –
a snare into which he who has sufficient respect for his dinner will rarely
fall.

WILLIAM MAGINN, *MAXIMS OF SIR WILLIAM O'DOHERTY, BART.*, 1849

Solid breakfasts are only fit for those who have much solid exercise to
take after it; otherwise heartburn may be looked for. Avoid new bread
and spongy rolls; look on muffins and crumpets as inventions of men
of worse than sanguinary principles, and hot buttered toast as of equally
wicked origin. Dry toast is the safest morning food, perhaps, for persons of indifferent powers of digestion.

DR JOHN DORAN, *TABLE TRAITS*, 1854

I think breakfasts so pleasant because no-one is conceited before one
o'clock.

SYDNEY SMITH IN *A MEMOIR OF THE REVD SYDNEY SMITH*
BY LADY HOLLAND, 1855

'Well, but I s'pose we may as well fall to,' observed his Lordship, cast-
ing his eye on the well-garnished table. 'All these good things are meant
to eat, I s'pose,' added he, '... cakes and sweets and jellies without end.
As to your sideboard... it's a match for any Lord Mayor's. A round of
beef, a goose, a ham or tongue, and is that a goose or a turkey?'

'A turkey, my Lord,' replied Springwheat; 'home-fed, my Lord.'

'Ah home-fed, indeed!' ejaculated his Lordship, with a shake of the
head; 'home-fed; wish I could feed at home. The man who said that

> E'en from the peasant to the Lord
> The turkey smokes on every board,

told a big 'un, for I'm sure none ever smokes on mine.'

'Take a little here today, then,' observed Mr Springwheat, cutting deep into the white breast.

'I will,' replied his Lordship. 'I will, and a slice of tongue, too,' added he.

'There are some hot sausingers comin',' observed Mr Springwheat.

'You don't say so!' replied his Lordship, apparently thunderstruck

at the announcement. 'Well, I must have all three. By Jove, Jack,' said he, appealing to his friend, 'but you've lit on your legs coming here today ... muffins and crumpets and cakes. Let me advise you to make the best use of your time, for you have but twenty minutes,' looking at his watch, 'and muffins and crumpets and cakes don't come your way every day.'

R. S. SURTEES, *MR SPONGE'S SPORTING TOUR*, 1853

The tea consumed was the very best, the coffee the very blackest, the cream the very thickest; there was dry toast and buttered toast, muffins and crumpets; hot bread and cold bread, white bread and brown bread, home-made bread and baker's bread, wheaten bread and oaten bread; and if there be other breads than these, they were there; there were eggs in napkins, and crispy bits of bacon under the silver covers; and there were little fishes in a little box, and devilled kidneys frizzling on a hot-water dish...

ANTHONY TROLLOPE, *THE WARDEN*, 1855

There is the low dark wainscoted room hung with sporting prints; the hat-stand (with a whip or two standing up in it belonging to bagmen who are still snug in bed), by the door; the blazing fire, with the quaint old glass over the mantelpiece, in which is stuck a large card with the list of the meets for the week of the county hounds. The table covered with the whitest of cloths and of china and bearing a pigeon-pie, ham, round of cold boiled beef cut from a mammoth ox, and the great loaf of household bread in a wooden trencher. And here comes in the stout head waiter, puffing under a tray of hot viands; kidneys and a steak, transparent rashers and poached eggs, buttered toast and muffins, coffee and tea, all smoking hot. The table can never hold it all; the cold meats are removed to the sideboard, they were only put on for show and to give us an appetite. And now fall on, gentlemen all.

THOMAS HUGHES, *TOM BROWN'S SCHOOLDAYS*, 1857

I never had a piece of toast
Particularly long and wide
But fell upon the sandy floor
And always on the buttered side.

JAMES PAYN IN *CHAMBERS' JOURNAL*, 1884

ODE TO THE LAST POT OF MARMALADE
To the fishers of Gjendin the bold Skipper spoke:
'There is one two-pound pot that as yet is unbroke;
So rouse ye, my gallants, and after our tea
Let us "go for" our Keiller's own Bonnie Dundee.'

(Chorus)
Come! up with the Smör! Come! out with the Brod,
We'll have one more Spise that's fit for a god;
Come, whip off the paper and let it gae free,
And we'll wade into Keiller's own Bonnie Dundee.

You may talk of your mölte with sugar and milk,
Your blueberry pasties, and jam of that ilk;
They are all very well in the wilds, don't you see?
But they can't hold a candle to Bonnie Dundee.

(Chorus as before)

Oh! the pies they were good, and the oven baked true,
With its door of green sod, and its sinuous flue,
Oh! the curry was toothsome as curry can be,
But where is the equal of Bonnie Dundee?

(Chorus again, gentlemen.)

There are ryper on Glopit as fleet as the wind,
And the Stor Bock roams on the Skagastolstind;
There are trout, teal, and woodcock, a sight for to see,
But what meal can be perfect without our Dundee?

(Chorus, if you please.)

Pandecagos are tasty, and omelettes are good;
Our eggs, though antique, not unsuited for food;
You can always be sure of at least one in three,
But blue mould cannot ruin our Bonnie Dundee.

(Chorus, only more so.)

31

Take my soup, though 'tis luscious, my öl, though 'tis rare,
My whisky, though scanty, beyond all compare;
Take my baccy, take all that is dearest to me,
But leave me one spoonful of Bonnie Dundee.

(Chorus ad lib.)

'JOHN', LATE NINETEENTH CENTURY

In England people try to be brilliant at breakfast. That is so dreadful of them! Only dull people are brilliant at breakfast.

OSCAR WILDE, *AN IDEAL HUSBAND*, 1895

He said firmly, 'Look here, gipsy! I tell you what we will do; and this is *my* last word. You shall hand me over six shillings and sixpence, cash down, and further, in addition thereto, you shall give me as much breakfast as I can possibly eat, at one sitting of course, out of that iron pot of yours that keeps sending forth such delicious and exciting smells. In return, I will make over to you my spirited young horse, with all the beautiful harness and trappings that are on him, freely thrown in. If that's not good enough for you, say so, and I'll be getting on. I know a man here who's wanted this horse of mine for years.

The gipsy grumbled frightfully, and declared if he did a few more deals of that sort he'd be ruined. But in the end he lugged a dirty canvas bag out of the depths of his trouser-pocket, and counted out six shillings and sixpence into Toad's paw. Then he disappeared into the caravan for an instant, and returned with a large iron plate and a knife, fork, and spoon. He tilted up the pot, and a glorious stream of hot rich stew gurgled into the plate. It was, indeed, the most beautiful stew in the world, being made of partridges, and pheasants, and chickens, and hares, and rabbits, and pea-hens, and guinea fowls, and one or two other things. Toad took the plate on his lap, almost crying, and stuffed, and stuffed, and stuffed, and stuffed, and kept asking for more, and the gipsy never grudged it him. He thought that he had never eaten so good a breakfast in all his life.

KENNETH GRAHAME, *THE WIND IN THE WILLOWS*, 1908

There is a vast difference between the savage and the civilised man, but it is never apparent to their wives until after breakfast.

HELEN ROWLAND, *A GUIDE TO MEN*

Adam ate some breakfast. No kipper, he reflected, is ever as good as it smells; how this too earthly contact with flesh and bone spoiled the first happy exhilaration; if only one could live, as Jehovah was said to have done, on the savour of burnt offerings. He lay back for a little in his bed thinking about the smells of food, of the greasy horror of fried fish and the deeply moving smell that came from it; of the intoxicating breath of bakeries and the dullness of buns...

EVELYN WAUGH, *VILE BODIES*, 1930

The following piece is from my old friend Ronnie Barker's autobiography. Ronnie, a brilliant comedian and writer, has been our friend since way back in 1957, when he and Annie toured together in a play called *Nekrassov*, which finished up at the Royal Court Theatre in Sloane Square. We had only recently been married and so had Ronnie and his wife Joy, so it was only natural that we felt drawn together. Since then Ronnie and I have also worked together, most notably in a romp called *The Seven Faces of Jim* with the legendary Jimmy Edwards, in which Ronnie and I had a hilarious time playing in a sketch about two lighthouse keepers. I only hope the audience enjoyed themselves half as much as we did! Later we appeared together in Tom Stoppard's play *The Real Inspector Hound*. Ronnie did a number of seasons at the Oxford Playhouse Theatre and Oxford has always been a special place for him.

This is my golden memory of Oxford, and always will be. My best time. If I were to pick the absolute quintessence of this time, it would be a May morning. On the first day of May, at six o'clock in the morning, the choir of Magdalen College gather on top of Magdalen Tower, which is on the banks of the river, and sing madrigals to welcome summer. The traffic, such as there was in those days, would stop or be stopped by the police, and the whole area would be hushed, silent. The clocks struck six and, high above us on the tower, the crystal voices would be heard, floating down to us on the still morning air. The people on the ground listened, breathless, to the crisp beauty of the church harmonies for perhaps fifteen or twenty minutes, and then silence; it was over. The place to listen was, of course, from a punt on the river. The water reflected the sound, so beautiful that it usually brought a tear or two to the eye.

After it was over, the breakfast-party would commence. We moved off downstream, and the girls in the group sorted out utensils and provisions. We moored the boat, set up an oil-stove in the meadow and cooked bacon, sausages and fried bread. Nothing ever before or since tasted as good as that May morning breakfast.

RONNIE BARKER, *DANCING IN THE MOONLIGHT*, 1993

This poem always makes us laugh: rationing reduced the most unlikely people to the most underhand ploys.

WEDDING BREAKFAST

In every part of the room, Matilda,
there are ladies who have come to wish you well.
They certainly do you credit; they are very elegant,
they are wearing the strangest hats and have clean gloves.
It is easy to see your friends are rich;
their dresses cost seventy-five pounds, their scent
was smuggled from Paris, their diamonds
glitter discreetly beneath their powdered throats.

But it may interest you to know, Matilda,
although of course you have no time for such things just now,
that one out of every three of these ladies
has managed (with the aid of a chiffon handkerchief
and a slight knowledge of legerdemain learned
in the schoolroom) to transfer
food from the buffet table into her handbag.
Lady Coppins has, at this moment, in her pocket
four chocolate biscuits which she has pinched for her son;
Corisande Broome has got hold of a little boat
filled with wet strawberries, and Lady de Witt
a meringue. These are now reposing
slightly tip-tilted, alas, but edible still,
next to the powder puffs and the Treasury notes:
loot to be carried back to the starving belovèds,
treasure for those who eat cakes made of sand at home,
creamily mixed with engagement books and gold pencils,
oozily leaning on letters and pots of rouge.

Dearest Matilda, we drink with delight to your future,
raising our glasses high in eternal salute,
and our glasses shall never be lowered until you are gone
lest the macaroons fall from the sleeves of our coats to the floor.

VIRGINIA GRAHAM, *PUNCH MAGAZINE*, JUNE 1948

BRITISH FOOD

Although I have been won over by certain aspects of international good living – French wines, Indian curries – in my heart of hearts I think of The Good Life as essentially an enjoyment of all that is best in British food and drink. The way to a man's heart is through his stomach and home is where the heart is, to coin a cliché or two.

Some years ago, during a Shakespearian world tour organized by the one and only Kenneth Branagh, we visited Tokyo, where, for me, it was difficult to find any decent food. I am the first to admit that I am not 'good at abroad' and only Ken could have got me this far from the Charing Cross Road. Annie is far more adventurous gastronomically than I am, and sampled raw fish with relish. Personally I just cannot understand why the Japanese don't bung all those excellent ingredients into a frying pan, and then we could all have a good meal. Why does raw fish require the services of a chef at all?

After a couple of days of virtual self-starvation one of my fellow actors informed me that there was a restaurant that served fried dishes. I was there like a shot. The food came, and there before me were several golden oblong shapes in thick batter. I cut the top off the first delicious-looking offering and out shot a claw – I didn't wait to find out what kind. After that I stuck to cheese sandwiches and Japan's finest – saki. I thoroughly recommend this as a winning combination when

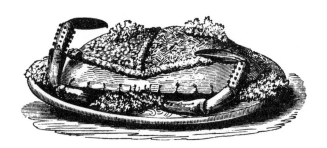

you cannot get hold of any of the goodies listed here so mouthwateringly by George Orwell. My own additions to Orwell's little list would include bacon and Marmite.

It is commonly said, even by the English themselves, that English cooking is the worst in the world. It is supposed to be not merely incompetent but imitative, and I even read quite recently, in a book by a French writer, the remark: 'The best English cooking is, of course, simply French cooking.'

Now that simply is not true. As anyone who has lived long abroad will know, there is a whole host of delicacies which it is quite impossible to obtain outside English-speaking countries. No doubt the list could be added to, but here are some of the things that I myself have sought for in foreign countries and failed to find.

First of all, kippers, Yorkshire pudding, Devonshire cream, muffins and crumpets. Then a list of puddings that would be interminable if I gave it in full: I will pick out for special mention Christmas pudding, treacle tart and apple dumplings. Then an almost equally long list of cakes: for instance, dark plum cake (such as you used to get at Buzzard's before the war), short-bread, and saffron buns. Also innumerable kinds of biscuit, which exist, of course, elsewhere, but are generally admitted to be better and crisper in England.

Then there are various ways of cooking potatoes that are peculiar to our own country. Where else do you see potatoes roasted under the joint, which is far and away the best way of cooking them? Or the delicious potato cakes that you get in the north of England? And it is far better to cook new potatoes in the English way – that is, boiled with mint and then served with a little melted butter or margarine – than to fry them as is done in most countries.

Then there are the various sauces peculiar to England. For instance, bread sauce, horse-radish sauce, mint sauce and apple sauce; not to mention redcurrant jelly, which is excellent with mutton as well as with hare, and various kinds of sweet pickle, which we seem to have in greater

profusion than most countries.

What else? Outside these islands I have never seen a haggis, except one that came out of a tin, nor Dublin prawns, nor Oxford marmalade, nor several other kinds of jam (marrow jam and bramble jelly, for instance), nor sausages of quite the same kind as ours.

Then there are the English cheeses. There are not many of them but I fancy that Stilton is the best cheese of its type in the world, with Wensleydale not far behind. English apples are also outstandingly good, particularly the Cox's Orange Pippin.

And finally, I would like to put in a word for English bread. All the bread is good, from the enormous Jewish loaves flavoured with caraway seeds to the Russian rye bread which is the colour of black treacle. Still, if there is anything quite as good as the soft part of the crust from an English cottage loaf (how soon shall we be seeing cottage loaves again?) I do not know of it.

GEORGE ORWELL, *EVENING STANDARD*, 1945

It is very remarkable, that in France, where there is but one religion, the sauces are infinitely varied, whilst in England, where the different sects are innumerable, there is, we may say, but one single sauce. Melted butter, in English cookery, plays nearly the same part as the Lord Mayor's coach at civic ceremonies, calomel in modern medicine, or silver forks in the fashionable novels. Melted butter and anchovies, melted butter and capers, melted butter and parsley, melted butter and eggs, and melted butter for ever.

LOUIS EUSTACHE UDE, *THE FRENCH COOK*, 1813

Oats. a grain which in England is generally given to horses, but in Scotland supports the people.

DR SAMUEL JOHNSON, *DICTIONARY OF THE ENGLISH LANGUAGE*, 1755

No, I can't eat oatcake; it is too rich for me.

SYDNEY SMITH

MULLY OF MOUNTOWN

Mountown! thou sweet retreat from Dublin cares,
Be famous for thy apples and thy pears;
For turnips, carrots, lettuce, beans and pease;
For Peggy's butter and for Peggy's cheese.
May clouds of pigeons round about thee fly!
But condescend sometimes to make a pie.
May fat geese gaggle with melodious voice,
And ne'er want gooseberries or apple sauce!
Ducks in thy ponds, and chickens in thy pens,
And be thy turkeys numerous as thy hens!
May thy black pigs lie warm in little sty,
And have no thought to grieve them till they die!
Mountown! the Muses' most delicious theme;
Oh! may thy codlins ever swim in cream!
Thy rasp- and straw- berries in Bourdeaux drown,
To add a redder tincture to their own!
Thy white-wine, sugar, milk, together club,
To make that gentle viand syllabub.
Thy tarts to tarts, cheese-cakes to cheese-cakes join,
To spoil the relish of the flowing wine.
But to the fading palate bring relief,
By thy Westphalian ham, or Belgic beef;
And, to complete thy blessings, in a word,
May still thy soil be generous as its lord!

WILLIAM KING, 1663–1712

CARVING

The termes of a Kerfer be as here followeth
Breke that dere – lesche that brawne – rere that goose – lyste that swanne
– sauce that capon – spoyle that hen – frusche that chekyn – unbrace
that mallarde – unlace that conye – dysmembre that heron – display
that crane – disfygure that peacocke – unjoynt that bytture – untache
that curlewe – alaye that fesande – wynge that partryche – wynge that
quayle – myne that plover – thye that pygyon – border that pasty – thye
that woodcocke – thye all maner smalle byrdes – tymbre that fyre –
tyere that egge – chynne that samon – strynge that lampreye – splat that
pyke – sauce that plaice – sauce that tench – splaye that breme – syde
that haddock – tuske that barbell – culpon that troute – fyne that cheven
– trassene that ele – trance that sturgeon – undertraunche that purpos
– tayme that crabbe – barbe that lopster – Here endeth the goodly termes of Kervynge.

WYNKYN DE WORDE, THE BOOKE OF KERVYNGE, 1508

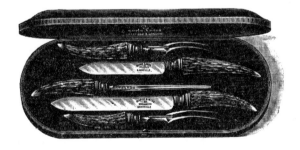

It may be stating the obvious but, in order to carve, it is essential to
have a sharp knife. We used to have a knife-grinder who turned up
on our doorstep, every six months or so, to sharpen our scissors and
knives. Sadly he does not come to our house any more; we fear that an
over-generous love of alcohol may have made the job a little too dan-

gerous for him – trembling hands and sharp knives do not make a good combination. Now I sharpen the knives, but the result is not as good.

Richard has always opted out of carving, so the task has fallen on me. I don't mind but I don't like being watched. This has led to a Christmas custom in our house of carving the turkey in the kitchen, before everyone comes to the table. It doesn't make such an impressive entrance but at least everything is served quickly and I don't have to keep repeating, 'Don't wait, do eat it while it's hot.' Nor do I risk depositing the unfortunate bird in a guest's lap; I doubt I would show the grace under pressure described in the following extract.

If you should, unhappily, be forced to carve, – neither labour at the joint until you put yourself into a heat, and hack it so that one might with justice exclaim, 'mangling done here!' nor make such a desperate effort to dissect it, as may put your neighbours in fear of their lives. However, if an accident should happen, make no excuses, for they are only an acknowledgment of awkwardness. We remember to have seen a man of high fashion deposit a turkey in this way in the lap of a lady; but, with admirable composure, and without offering the slightest apology, he finished a story which he was telling at the same time, and then, quietly turning to her, merely said – 'Madam, I'll thank you for that turkey.'

LAUNCELOT STURGEON, *ESSAYS, MORAL, PHILOSOPHICAL AND STOMACHICAL, ON THE IMPORTANT SCIENCE OF GOOD-LIVING*, 1822

CHAMPAGNE

Champagne had always been a bit of a mystery to me. I don't mean the taste, I mean the price. Why is it only a few pounds cheaper than the great Bushmills Irish whiskey, which can keep you happy for about three days? They say it's an expensive process producing the bubbles and I suppose it must be. Nevertheless it is a cast-iron seller. Weddings, christenings, funerals all demand that you have it. It is a mark of your position, your measure of success, the achievement of The Good Life. Incidentally, another mystery to me is why sportspersons always spray

champagne around and over each other when they win an event.

Having previously rather knocked champers, my eyes were opened after one extremely happy encounter with it. We had invited Albert Finney, our old friend from RADA days, over for lunch on his fiftieth birthday. With his usual generosity he had brought with him a noble bottle of Dom Pérignon, which is, of course, a very different thing altogether. It was amazing – a revelation to my cynical self – and proved once again the sorry fact that in this life you only get what you pay for.

'Champagne isn't worth a copper unless it's iced – is it Colonel?'

'Vy, I don't know – I carn't say I like it so werry cold; it makes my teeth chatter, and cools my courage as it gets below – champagne certainly gives one werry gentlemanly ideas, but for a continuance, I don't know but I should prefer mild hale.'

R. S. Surtees, *Jorrocks's Jaunts and Jollities*, 1838

Algernon. Why is it that at a bachelor's establishment the servants invariably drink the champagne? I ask merely for information.

Lane. I attribute it to the superior quality of the wine, sir. I have often observed that in married households the champagne is rarely of a first-rate brand.

Oscar Wilde, *The Importance of Being Earnest*, 1895

Champagne is art's greatest triumph over nature, a civilized wine that must be drunk in civilized conditions; the Chopin among wines. We do not expect of it the elemental surge of Burgundy, nor the austerity of claret. To drink it throughout a dinner suggests a menu designed for ladies, no red meats nor advanced game blend with its rococo appeal.

It is a drawing-room wine, as Chopin was the supreme composer for this setting – a room, we sometimes feel, a little over-heated and scented; a room in which the decoration seems to exist for its own sake ...

As a tonic it is, of course, the swiftest and most pleasant of all...

Cheap champagne is a deadly potion, one that the Borgias must regret was created too late for their use. Nearly all reliable wine merchants, however, supply a reasonable brand of their own 'reserve' at nine or ten shillings a bottle, and in such cases no damage need be feared.

EDWARD AND LORNA BUNYARD, *THE EPICURE'S COMPANION*, 1937

CHEESE

Despite dire warnings about cholesterol, migraines and bad dreams Richard and I love cheese and never miss an opportunity to try out a new variety. Our local delicatessen has introduced us to several, including Manchego, a Spanish cheese that is perfectly delicious eaten with a very small dollop of membrillo (quince paste). I used to tease my father for liking a teaspoonful of jam with his Cheddar or Cheshire cheese but now I wonder if there isn't an unknown Spanish ancestor lurking in our family's past.

For part of my childhood we lived in Chester, and I can still clearly remember the huge rounds of white or coral-coloured Cheshire cheese displayed on the stalls of the indoor market next to the Town Hall. I was gratified many years later to discover that Mrs Beeton described Cheshire cheese as 'famed all over Europe for its rich quality and fine piquant flavour'.

In 1991 Richard and I were in Tuscany, for the filming of *Much Ado About Nothing*. Whenever I was free I used to drive down a winding hill, through the beautiful sun-warmed countryside, to the market in the little country town of Greve. Being *much* further south than Chester the market did not need to be under cover, and the stalls were set up in the open air. Twice a week in the market square, surrounded by little shops and cafés, the stalls were piled high with goods and provisions: sheets and pillowcases, shoes, T-shirts, jeans, electrical items, fruit and vegetables, and, of course, local cheese. Mostly it was Parmesan; not the small, genteel segments we get in Britain but huge, pale-yellow craggy cliffs of it laid out on the tables. Older men in dark jackets, older women in black or floral dresses, and young people in jeans and T-shirts would buy the

Parmesan in great big chunks, while our group stood in the sunshine, tasting. It crumbled a little as it went into the mouth and was utterly wonderful. It makes my mouth water just to think of it, and the thought takes me straight back to Tuscany.

Cheese and bread for gentlemen,
Corn and hay for horses,
Tobacco for the old wives,
And kisses for the lasses.

TRADITIONAL

It is well known that some persons like cheese in a state of decay, and even 'alive'. There is no accounting for taste, and it may be hard to show why mould, which is vegetation, should not be eaten as well as salad, or maggots as well as eels. But, generally speaking, decomposing bodies are not wholesome eating, and the line must be drawn somewhere.

MRS BEETON, *MRS BEETON'S BOOK OF HOUSEHOLD MANAGEMENT*, 1861

RAREBIT *n.* A Welsh rabbit, in the speech of the humorless, who point out that it is not a rabbit. To whom it may be solemnly explained that the comestible known as toad-in-the-hole is really not a toad, and that riz-de-veau à la financière is not the smile of a calf prepared after the recipe of a she banker.

AMBROSE BIERCE, *THE DEVIL'S DICTIONARY*, 1911

It is cant to say that a Welsh rabbit is heavy eating... I like it best in the genuine Welsh way, however – that is, the toasted bread buttered on both sides profusely, then a layer of cold roast-beef, with mustard and horse-raddish, and then, on the top of all, the superstratum of Cheshire *thoroughly* saturated, while in the process of toasting, with cwrw, or, in its absence, porter, genuine porter, black pepper, and shallot vinegar. I peril myself upon the assertion, that this is not a heavy supper for a man who has been busy all day till dinner, in reading, writing, walking, or riding – who has occupied himself between dinner and supper in the discussion of a bottle or two of sound wine, or any equivalent – and who proposes to swallow at least three tumblers of something hot, ere he resigns himself to the embrace of Somnus.

WILLIAM MAGINN, *MAXIMS OF SIR WILLIAM O'DOHERTY, BART.*, 1849

Cheese is milk that has grown up.

EDWARD AND LORNA BUNYARD, *THE EPICURE'S COMPANION*, 1937

'When a woman asks for back, I call her "madam",' said a grocer. 'When she asks for streaky I call her "dear". You can always tell the gentry,' he went on, 'by their knowledge of cheese. They don't have trouble saying the foreign names.'

JILLY COOPER, *CLASS*, 1980

CHOCOLATE AND SWEETS

I have to confess that I remember quite clearly the days of wartime sweet-rationing. Perhaps that particular piece of legislation should have been continued for the good of the nation's teeth and waistlines. Succumbing to those colourfully wrapped, mouthwatering treats is for most of us our first self-indulgence in life. I remember my grandmother saying that her idea of heaven was a night out at the theatre with a box of chocs and the two Jacks (heart-throbs Buchanan and Hulbert). One of my favourite quotations, expressing remarkably similar sentiments, is Noël Coward's throwaway remark: 'My idea of a good afternoon's exercise is fifty Turkish cigarettes and a box of marrons glacés.'

I never believed that chocolate was addictive until some years ago when I was in an Ayckbourn play with Sheila Hancock. One evening she burst into my dressing room brandishing a large box of chocolates that had been given to her by a fan, and demanded that I lock them away in my cupboard and allow her only one a day.

'That's a bit extreme Sheila,' I said. 'I mean, I know you're usually on *some* health kick but...'

'You don't understand!' she cried. 'I can finish a pound of the damn things in ten minutes!'

49

She was, of course, a member of that unfortunate breed, the chocoholic. So be warned.

There was a period when I became a toffeeholic. Fine during carefree youth, with a mouthful of sturdy teeth; less agreeable in middle age, when years of happy chewing have left you with a mouth filled with plastic. Believe me, I know!

19 June 1662

And then with the last chest of Crusados to Alderman Backwells; by the same token, his lady, going to take coach, stood in the shop and having a gilded glassful of perfumed confits given her by Don Duarte de Silva, the Portugall merchant that is come over with the Queene, I did offer at a taste, and so she poured some out into my hand; and though good, yet pleased me the better coming from a pretty lady.

SAMUEL PEPYS, *DIARY*

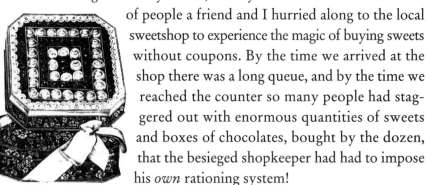

While Richard and I were chewing over our childhood recollections of sweets, I was reminded of the momentous day when sweet-rationing eventually ended, some years after the war. Like a lot of people a friend and I hurried along to the local sweetshop to experience the magic of buying sweets without coupons. By the time we arrived at the shop there was a long queue, and by the time we reached the counter so many people had staggered out with enormous quantities of sweets and boxes of chocolates, bought by the dozen, that the besieged shopkeeper had had to impose his *own* rationing system!

For both of us the following piece by Audrey Earle took us right back to our own pocket-money days.

Our own brother used to spend his weekly pocket money, one penny, on an ounce of the best milk chocolate and cram it all into his mouth at once, saying he liked *one good taste*. My sister and I preferred quantity to quality and felt it rather hard that he should then expect us to share our sweets with him when he had nothing to offer in exchange. Golden pralines with a mushy centre were a favourite, but fruit-drops went further and humbugs, striped like zebras, lasted longest of all and were so hot that one had to move them hastily from one cheek to the other. Then there were little bags of sherbet, four a penny, with a hollow black liquorice stick through which one drew it up till it fizzed in one's mouth and tickled the throat pleasantly. Once I purchased some tiny silver balls which were fashionable then for decorating wedding cakes, but they were a great disappointment, the silver sucked off at once and the minute ball, highly scented with peppermint, was difficult to anchor. In truth I felt like the poor man at the Old Folks' Dinner making slow going, who, when asked if anything were wrong, replied, 'Oive only one tooth and oi be trying to spear pickled oonion with it.'

AUDREY EARLE IN *A WINE AND FOOD BEDSIDE BOOK*, 1972

CHRISTMAS AND OTHER FESTIVALS

F amily Christmas: preparations for this event can be nerve-racking, exhausting and expensive. Your perennial hope is that the look of joy on the faces of your loved ones as they troop through the front door will make it all worth while. As a precaution I recommend you have one really stiff drink just before they hove into sight.

In the early days, before Annie had taken over the Christmas arrangements, we used to travel to my parents' house for the festive lunch. On one occasion my father, who did the cooking, having had one dry sherry too many on Christmas Eve, had overslept and was late putting the bird in the oven. Panic had set in and on our arrival we were greeted at the door by a large Dad, face bedewed by perspiration, still in an ancient dressing-gown secured in the middle by an enormous safety pin and brandishing a carving knife as he uttered the immortal words: 'It's a total disaster, but we've got to enjoy ourselves – it *is* bloody Christmas!'

Ah! happy days, though somewhat removed from Trollope's idealized picture of the scene.

They all went to church, as a united family ought to do on Christmas Day, and came home to a fine old English early dinner at three o'clock, – a sirloin of beef a foot and a half broad, a turkey as big as an ostrich, a plum-pudding bigger than the turkey, and two or three dozen mince-pies.

ANTHONY TROLLOPE, *CHRISTMAS AT THOMPSON HALL*, 1876

When Richard and I were just married, and acting jobs were thin on the ground, we used to read the hilarious Geoffrey Willans books *How to be Topp* and *Down with Skool!* to cheer ourselves up. Best of all we used to read them out aloud to each other, and always ended up roaring with laughter. We've included this piece about Christmas not just because it is so funny and true – especially the punchline – but also because it reminds us of what was a very happy time, despite all the problems that are inevitable when you are struggling young actors.

Xmas day always starts badly becos molesworth 2 blub he hav not got the reel rools-royce he asked for. We then hav argument that each hav more presents than the other. A Mery Xmas everybode sa scrooge in the end but we just call each other clot-faced wets so are you you you you pointing with our horny fingers it is very joly i must sa. In the end i wear molesworth 2's cowboy suit and he pla with my air gun so all is quiet.

Then comes DINNER.

This is super as there are turkey crackers nuts cream plum puding jely and everything. We wash it down with a litle ginger ale but grown ups all drink wine ugh and this make all the old lades and grans very sprightly i must sa. They sa how sweet we are they must be dotty until pater raps the table and look v. solemn. He holds up his glass and sa in a low voice

The QUEEN. Cheers cheers cheers for the queen we all drink and hurra for england.

Then pater sa in much lower voice ABSENT FRIENDS and everyone else sa absent friends absent friends ect. and begin blubbing. In fact it do not seme that you can go far at xmas time without blubbing of some sort...

Stil xmas is a good time with all those presents and good food and i hope it will never die out or at any rate not until i am grown up and hav to pay for it all.

GEOFFREY WILLANS, *How To Be Topp*, 1954

As they approached the farm their song changed to:

> Harvest home! Harvest home!
> Merry, merry, merry harvest home!
> Our bottles are empty, our barrels won't run,
> And we think it's a very dry harvest home.

and the farmer came out, followed by his daughters and maids with jugs and bottles and mugs, and drinks were handed round amidst general

ENGLISH HARVEST-HOME.

congratulations. Then the farmer invited the men to his harvest home dinner, to be held in a few days' time, and the adult workers dispersed to add up their harvest money and to rest their weary bones…

On the morning of the harvest home dinner everybody prepared themselves for a tremendous feast, some to the extent of going without breakfast, that the appetite might not be impaired. And what a feast it was! Such a bustling in the farmhouse kitchen for days beforehand; such boiling of hams and roasting of sirloins; such a stacking of plum puddings, made by the Christmas recipe; such a tapping of eighteen-gallon casks and baking of plum loaves would astonish those accustomed to the appetites of today. By noon the whole parish had assembled, the workers and their wives and children to feast and the sprinkling of the better-to-do to help with the serving. The only ones absent were the aged bedridden and their attendants, and to them, the next day, portions, carefully graded in daintiness according to their social standing, were carried by the children from the remnants of the feast. A plum pudding was considered a delicate compliment to an equal of the farmer; slices of beef or ham went to the 'bettermost poor'; and a ham-bone with plenty of meat left upon it or part of a pudding or a can of soup to the commonalty.

Long tables were laid out of doors in the shade of a barn, and soon after twelve o'clock the cottagers sat down to the good cheer, with the farmer carving at the principal table, his wife with her tea urn at another, the daughters of the house and their friends circling the tables with vegetable dishes and beer jugs, and the grandchildren, in their stiff, white, embroidered frocks, dashing hither and thither to see that everybody had what they required. As a background there was the rick-yard with its new yellow stacks and, over all, the mellow sunshine of late summer.

FLORA THOMPSON, *LARK RISE TO CANDLEFORD*, 1945

AUTUMN'S HARVEST
Who ate the first blackberry?
I did, I ate the first blackberry,
Its flesh was sweet,
Like a glossy, purple clot.

Who cracked the first hazelnut?
The small mouse-brown spheres,
Crunchy, with a lustful taste,
A real harvest treat.

When will the damsons fall from the tree?
Their stalks so thin, like a spider's spin,
The juice like thickened harvest wine,
Leaving stains upon the tongue.

Who picked the last apple?
I did, I picked the last apple,
Autumn's blood was in it,
Like a rose red globe.

TIM GILBERT, © 1986

56

BIRTHDAY PARTY

Against my birth-day thou shalt be my guest:
Weele haue Greene-cheeses and fine Silly-bubs;
And thou shalt be the chiefe of all my feast.
And I will giue thee two fine pretie Clubs,
With two young Whelps, to make thee sport with all,
A golden Racket and a Tennis-ball.

A guilded Nutmeg, and a race of Ginger,
A silken Girdle, and a drawn-worke Band,
Cuffs for thy wrists, a gold Ring for thy finger,
And sweet Rose-water for thy Lilly-white hand.
A Purse of silke, bespanged with spots of gold,
As braue a one as ere thou didst behold.

A paire of Kniues, a greene Hat and a Feather,
New gloues to put vpon thy milk-white hand
Ile giue thee, for to keep thee from the weather;
With Phoenix feathers shall thy face be fand,
Cooling those Cheekes, that being cool'd wexe red,
Like Lillyes in a bed of Roses shed.

RICHARD BARNFIELD, 1594

———

We both found John McCarthy's account of his years as a hostage
in Beirut extremely moving. There are so many simple pleasures
we take for granted, and the extraordinary way in which the hostages
coped with the loss of freedom and privacy as well as a lack of basic
food and amenities was amazing. Yet even in those extreme conditions
there were lighter moments and opportunities for humour.

———

The day after the interrogation, Ali came in and gave me a pair of pyja-
mas. I put them on, he sprinkled perfume over me and led me out with

Bri to the guards' room. He set us down on the floor with Ayeesa, Sayeed and the others. He raised my blindfold a little to show me the spread of cake, fruit and sweets. 'This is Happy Birthday for you.'

I was flabbergasted. I'd hoped yet dreaded that they wanted me to make a video. Why else would they be dressing me up? We knew that Anderson had been photographed with a birthday cake and shown a video of his little daughter Salome, born since his kidnap. But this was just a party. The guards made a dreadful racket, singing 'Happy Birthday' with Brian. It was extraordinary that they enforced quietness at all times so that the hostages in their cells shouldn't hear one another yet now they were bellowing an English song with an Irish baritone flowing free over the top of them. Then Brian explained that it was a tradition in Ireland for the birthday guest to make a speech. Sayeed therefore called on me to make one.

'Well, I'd like to thank you all for having a party for me. I wish I could thank you face to face. I have only ever seen your feet but they look like good feet and I hope you are good men and that this will be the only birthday where we have to sit like this unable to look at each other properly.'

JOHN MCCARTHY IN JOHN MCCARTHY AND JILL MORRELL,
SOME OTHER RAINBOW, 1993

I've always had a fondness for Samuel Pepys and his idiosyncratic diary. Pepys was an enthusiastic theatre-goer, although somewhat inclined to make disparaging remarks about what he saw, particularly if the play was by Shakespeare. Here he is on a production he saw on 1 March 1662: '*Romeo and Juliet* is a play, of itself, the worst that ever I heard in my life, and worse acted than ever I saw these people do.' I'm grateful never to have been on the receiving end of one of his succinct reviews; no wonder Nell Gwynne gave up the stage.

Pepys knew how to enjoy himself and never missed an opportunity to party. All the usual festivals were celebrated, but in his personal annual calendar there was a unique celebration: the anniversary of the day when 'the Stone' was removed. Not a very jolly experience even with all the benefits of modern medicine, it must have been a fairly appalling procedure more than three hundred years ago. Having survived, Pepys kept his own festival every year as a reminder of just how good it was to be alive and well.

4 April 1663
By and by comes Roger Pepys, Mrs Turner, her daughter, Joyce Norton and a young lady, a daughter of Collonell Cockes – my uncle Wight – his wife and Mrs Anne Wight – this being my feast, in lieu of what I should have had a few days ago, for my cutting of the Stone, for which the Lord make me truly thankful.

Very merry before, at, and after dinner, and the more for that my dinner was great and most neatly dressed by our own only mayde. We had a fricasse of rabbets and chicken – a leg of mutton boiled – three carps in a dish – a great dish of a side of lamb – a dish of roasted pigeons – a dish of four lobsters – three tarts – a Lampry pie, a most rare pie – a dish of anchoves – good wine of several sorts; and all things most noble and to my great content.

SAMUEL PEPYS, *DIARY*

COCKTAILS

I think we are both more enamoured of the *idea* of a cocktail than the actuality. The very word conjures up an aura of sophistication and elegance – very grown-up, very Noël Coward.

We are both also great fans of Ogden Nash: we love his sense of humour and clever way with words. The following poem, with its air of ingenuous surprise that alcohol might actually be the secret ingredient, always reminds us of a marvellous visit to Washington and our first mint julep. Never having been great connoisseurs of the more esoteric cocktails, we thought that the capital of the United States might be a promising place in which to try out some of the delights less easily available on our home shores. Thus we confidently ordered a brace of mint juleps from the barman at a very upmarket Washington hotel, without having the remotest idea what would turn up. Clearly neither did the barman, for to our great surprise the poor man looked horrorstruck, scuttled away and didn't re-emerge for about half an hour. When he *did*

reappear he brought the most wonderful concoction, which we sipped with a nonchalant and knowing air. And my word it really was good. Whether it was a true mint julep or not we were never certain. Anyway, in case you should ever find yourselves in a similar situation, here is a mint julep recipe to keep about your person for the benefit of confused barmen the world over.

Southern Mint Julep
4 sprigs fresh young mint
½ tablespoon caster sugar
1 scant tablespoon plain water
1 generous measure Bourbon or rye whiskey
mint for decoration

Crush the mint leaves and sugar together with the water in a long tumbler until the sugar is fairly well dissolved. Add the whiskey. Fill the glass with cracked ice. Stir very gently until the glass is frosted. Serve decorated with a sprig of fresh mint.

A Drink with Something in It
There is something about a martini,
A tingle remarkably pleasant;
A yellow, a mellow martini;
I wish that I had one at present.
There is something about a martini,

Ere the dining and dancing begin,
And to tell you the truth,
It is not the vermouth –
I think that perhaps it's the gin.

There is something about an old-fashioned
That kindles a cardiac glow;
It is soothing and soft and impassioned
As a lyric by Swinburne or Poe.
There is something about an old-fashioned
When dusk has enveloped the sky,
And it may be the ice,
Or the pineapple slice,
But I strongly suspect it's the rye.

There is something about a mint julep.
It is nectar imbibed in a dream,
As fresh as the bud of a tulip,
As cool as the bed of a stream.
There is something about a mint julep,
A fragrance beloved by the lucky.
And perhaps it's the tint
Of the frost and the mint,
But I think it was born in Kentucky.

There is something they put in a highball
That awakens the torpidest brain,
That kindles a spark in the eyeball,
Gliding singing through vein after vein.
There is something they put in a highball
Which you'll notice one day, if you watch;
And it may be the soda,
But judged by the odor,
I rather believe it's the scotch.

Then here's to the heartening wassail,
Wherever good fellows are found;
Be its master instead of its vassal,
And order the glasses around.
For there's something they put in the wassail
That prevents it from tasting like wicker,
Since it's not tapioca,
Or mustard, or mocha,
I'm forced to conclude it's the liquor.

OGDEN NASH

I must get out of these wet clothes and into a dry Martini.

ALEXANDER WOOLLCOTT (ATTR.)

COFFEE

Why do they always put mud into coffee onboard steamers? Why does tea generally taste of boiled boots?

WILLIAM MAKEPEACE THACKERAY, *THE KICKLEBURYS ON THE RHINE*, 1850

The ritual that surrounded making coffee in the eighteenth century, when beans were roasted and ground in the drawing room, is described in this poem. The respect shown for this delicious drink is a good reminder of what a treat real, fresh coffee is. Certainly not something to be taken for granted.

For lo! the board with cups and spoons is crown'd,
The berries crackle, and the mill turns round:
On shining altars of Japan they raise
The silver lamp; the fiery spirits blaze:
From silver spouts the grateful liquors glide,
While China's earth receives the smoking tide:
At once they gratify their scent and taste,
And frequent cups prolong the rich repast.
Straight hover round the fair her airy band;
Some, as she sipp'd, the fuming liquor fann'd,
Some o'er her lap their careful plumes display'd,
Trembling, and conscious of the rich brocade.
Coffee (which makes the politician wise,

And see through all things with his half-shut eyes)
Sent up in vapours to the baron's brain
New strategems, the radiant lock to gain.

ALEXANDER POPE, *THE RAPE OF THE LOCK*, 1714

I did make coffee once, after sendin' out for instructions. But then I got otherwise involved in somethin' more interestin' and forgot to turn off the heat. Well – I never turn off the heat.

MAE WEST

CONVERSATION

There must, in the first place, be knowledge; there must be materials. In the second place, there must be a command of words; in the third place, there must be imagination, to place things in such a view as they are not commonly seen in; and, in the fourth place, there must be presence of mind, and a resolution that is not overcome by failures. This last is an essential requisite; for want of it many people do not excel in conversation. Now, *I* want it; I throw up the game upon losing a trick.

DR JOHNSON IN JAMES BOSWELL, *LIFE OF SAMUEL JOHNSON*, 1791

The English appear to prefer the bottle to the society of ladies. This is illustrated by dismissing the ladies from the table and remaining for

hours to drink and intoxicate themselves. If I were in England I should certainly leave the table with the ladies. If the object is to talk instead of to drink, why banish them? Surely, conversation is never so lively nor so witty as when ladies take a part in it.

NAPOLEON IN DE BOURIENNE, *PRIVATE MEMOIRS OF NAPOLEON*

IN CONVERSATION, TRIFLING OCCURRENCES, such as small disappoint-ments, petty annoyances, and other everyday incidents, should never be mentioned to friends. A bad habit that very many people get into is to tattle of their servants and children incessantly, not realising that to many of their listeners they are most wearisome subjects, while to most they are very uninteresting ones. The extreme injudiciousness of repeat-ing these will be at once apparent when we reflect on the unsatisfactory discussions they too frequently occasion, and the load of advice which may, thereupon, be tendered, and which is too often neither useful nor agreeable. Greater events, whether of joy or sorrow, should be com-municated to friends; and, on such occasions, their sympathy gratifies and comforts. If the mistress be a wife never let a word, in connection with her husband's failures, pass her lips; and in cultivating the power of conversation, she should keep the versified counsel of Cowper con-tinually in her memory, – that it

'Should flow like water after summer showers
Not as if raised by mere mechanic powers.'

The secret of our conversation being entertaining or the reverse consists mainly of suiting it to that of those with whom we are speaking. To some it is necessary to say very little at all, for they much prefer to talk themselves, and it is the duty of the hostess to listen as sympathetically or as interestedly as she can. Other people are shy, and then a good deal of tact is required to find out what would be pleasant subjects for them, for there are sure to be some upon which they can speak, and it is well for the mistress of a household to learn as much as she can of the leading topics of the day.

MRS BEETON, *MRS BEETON'S BOOK OF HOUSEHOLD MANAGEMENT*, 1861

Murder is always a mistake... One should never do anything that one cannot talk about after dinner.

OSCAR WILDE, *THE PICTURE OF DORIAN GRAY*, 1891

Aldred had never been to school before, but she was so happy at the Grange that she was sure no other place in the United Kingdom could

be half so nice. Miss Drummond was certainly a delightful head mistress... She would discuss topics of the day, books, music, art, or any other subject with her pupils, trying to make them talk easily and naturally, and take an intelligent interest in what was going on in the world.

'Conversation is like a game of ball,' she would sometimes say; 'it must be thrown backwards and forwards from both sides. There is nothing so aggravating as to be obliged to talk to a person who will persist in only answering with a negative or an affirmative. I have racked my brains sometimes to think of fresh topics, when all my leading remarks have been received with a "Yes" or a "No". That is what I call dropping the ball. When you see people are making an effort to entertain you, it is only fair to play your part well. I know you plead shyness but shyness can be conquered if we try to forget ourselves, and think only how we can give pleasure to others.'

ANGELA BRAZIL, *A FOURTH FORM FRIENDSHIP*, 1911

1940 October 16 Wednesday
Dined last night at the Randolph with Archie Macdonell, his wife, and Leslie Banks. The menu, which was the ordinary hotel dinner, much too elaborate for war time. Hors d'oeuvres, choice of soup, sweetbreads, partridge, sweet and savoury. An admirable bottle of Pommard, a lot of good talk, and, what is rarer, good listening. Archie said that the best talk immediately before the war was to be heard in Fleet Street during the lunch hour and at the table reserved for Bevan Wyndham-Lewis, Johnny Morton, James Bone, Douglas Woodruff, and Hilaire Belloc. He was too modest to include himself, though he might have done... Told us that the wittiest impromptu he had ever heard was Bevan's description of Mistinguett as 'A rose-red cutie half as old as Time.'

JAMES AGATE, *EGO 6*

COOKS AND COOKERY

We may live without poetry, music and art;
We may live without conscience, and live without heart;
We may live without friends; we may live without books;
But civilized man cannot live without cooks.

EDWARD BULWER-LYTTON, *LUCILE*, 1803–73

Cookery means the knowledge of Medea and Circe, and of Helen and the Queen of Sheba. It means the knowledge of all herbs and fruits and balms and spices and all that is healing and sweet in the fields and the groves, and savoury in meats.

It means carefulness and inventiveness and willingness and readiness of appliances.

It means the economy of your grandmothers and the science of the modern chemist; it means much tasting and no wasting; it means English thoroughness and French art, and Arabian hospitality...

JOHN RUSKIN 1819–1900

Kissing don't last: cookery do!

GEORGE MEREDITH, *THE ORDEAL OF RICHARD FEVEREL*, 1859

Progress in civilization has been accompanied by progress in cookery.

FANNIE FARMER, BOSTON *COOKING SCHOOL COOKBOOK*, 1896

Cooking is like love – it should be entered into with abandon, or not at all.

HARRIET VAN HORNE, QUOTED IN *VOGUE*, 1956

Plain cooking cannot be entrusted to plain cooks.

COUNTESS MORPHY

The cook was a good cook, as cooks go; and as cooks go she went.

SAKI, *REGINALD ON BESETTING SINS*, 1904

There was a fellow I stayed with once in Warwickshire who farmed his own land, but was otherwise quite steady. Should never have suspected him of having a soul, yet not very long afterwards he eloped with a lion-

tamer's widow and set up as a golf instructor somewhere on the Persian Gulf; dreadfully immoral, of course, because he was only an indifferent player, but still, it showed imagination. His wife was really to be pitied, because he had been the only person in the house who understood how to manage the cook's temper, and now she has to put 'D.V.' on her dinner invitations. Still, that's better than a domestic scandal; a woman who leaves her cook never wholly recovers her position in Society.

SAKI, *REGINALD ON HOUSE-PARTIES*, 1904

ASKING FOR CHARACTER OF COOK

The Gables,
Whitby.
May 10, 19–.

Madam, –

Lucy Thomas, who has applied to me for the situation as cook in my household, tells me that she has lived with you for three and a half years, and that you will give her a character.

Will you kindly tell me if she understands her work? I require a really experienced cook, and one I can rely on. Is she clean, and honest, and steady?

I shall be greatly honoured by an answer to the above questions.

Yours truly,

J. Roberts.

FAVOURABLE

Dorset Mansions,
Orchard Street,
May 11, 19–,

Madam, –

Lucy Thomas gave me the greatest satisfaction during the three years and a half she lived with me, and I only parted with her because I was giving up housekeeping.

She is a thoroughly good cook, is clean and honest, and quite trustworthy.

Yours truly,
T. A. Murdoch.

UNFAVOURABLE

Dorset Mansions,
Orchard Street,
May 11, 19–,

Madam, –

Lucy Thomas is a perfectly honest, clean and trustworthy servant, but her skill in cooking is not great. I kept her for three years and more hoping she would improve, but she did not. If you required a plain cook only she would do excellently, and she is a very good servant in every other respect.

Yours truly,
T. A. Murdoch.

RONALD PELHAM, *HOW SHALL I WORD IT? A COMPLETE LETTER WRITER FOR MEN AND WOMEN*

A good cook is like a sorceress who dispenses happiness.

ELSA SCHIAPARELLI, 1890–1973

Neither knowledge nor diligence can create a great chef. What use is conscientiousness as a substitute for inspiration?

COLETTE

All good cooks, like all great artists, must have an audience worth cooking for or singing to.

ANDRÉ SIMON, FOUNDER OF THE WINE AND FOOD SOCIETY, 1933

CURRIES

A cook named McMurray
Got a raise in a hurry
From his Hindu employer
By favoring curry.

OGDEN NASH, *VERSUS*, 1949

I consumed my first curry at about the age of four. My grandparents
had lived in India for years before returning to England in 1930,
so curries made regular appearances on the lunch and dinner tables. I
wasn't too keen at first and preferred the side dishes, especially cha-
patis which I scoffed at tea-time covered somewhat unconventionally
with strawberry jam. During the war Indian dishes came into their
own because small quantities of meat and chicken could be eked out
with large helpings of dhal and rice at almost every meal.

Later on I experimented with adventurous dishes in Indian restaurants. I slowly built up my 'heat intake' from korma (mild), through
Madras (medium hot) to vindaloo (hot), without disastrous results.
Unfortunately one particular evening, under the influence of draught
Bass, I ordered a chicken phal (Very Hot) and regretted it at once. Phal
is pronounced 'farl' and that is not unlike the sound you emit after the
second mouthful, just before you gasp for immediate medical attention.
The antidote is to eat bread, which scrapes the molten substance off
your tongue; or chocolate, which is surprisingly effective.

Sadly, as I have grown older I find I can only really eat curry at
lunchtime. Eaten late at night it leads to a restless night in which I seem
to spend eight hours being chased by Alsatians and sliding off precip-
itous cliffs.

The most amazing Indian meal I ever enjoyed was one produced by

the much-loved Felicity Kendal during the making of *The Good Life*, in which we played husband and wife. Felicity and her family had lived for years in India, where they were a famous theatrical troupe who toured the sub-continent giving performances of Shakespeare's plays.

The meal was fantastic, a real banquet with wonderful flavours I had never tasted before. Felicity's sister Jennifer was still in Bombay and had sent over a jar of home-made garlic and chilli chutney as a gift for the evening's celebrations. We dug into this with great relish. Innocuous at first, on reaching the stomach the delayed-action chillies were activated and there was a kind of detonation as the chillies and the garlic met in wild collision. It was actually rather sensational, but the after-effects were long lasting: it was a week before my breath stopped reeking of garlic and I could be accepted back into the community.

ANNIE'S VEGETABLE CURRY
*Serves 2–3 accompanied by rice (Basmati if possible) or 4 if also
served with a side dish such as dhal.*

*1½ lb (700 g) mixed vegetables, chopped (I use a mixture of yellow and green
peppers, fennel, aubergine, carrots, courgettes and cooked beetroot. You can
use whatever is available but potatoes, green beans and peas are also good.)*

4 tablespoons vegetable oil
1 teaspoon mustard seeds
1 small–medium onion, chopped
½–1 green chilli and/or 1 Carib chilli (yellow and mild) chopped
1–2 garlic cloves, finely chopped
2–3 teaspoons grated fresh ginger
1½ teaspoons ground turmeric
1 tablespoon ground coriander
¼ teaspoon cayenne pepper
2 cloves
1 bayleaf
*1 small tin chopped tomatoes or equivalent volume fresh tomatoes, skinned
and chopped*
approx 5 fl. oz (150 ml) water
2–3 tablespoons desiccated coconut
2 generous tablespoons fresh coriander, finely chopped

Heat the oil in a large, heavy frying pan or casserole, over a high heat. Add the mustard seeds, taking care that they do not spit at you. Almost immediately, turn the heat down, add the onion, chilli and garlic and fry gently for a few minutes. Add the grated ginger, turmeric, ground coriander and cayenne, stir and cook for 1 minute. (If you prefer a mild curry you can leave out the green chilli, and for a very mild curry omit the cayenne pepper as well.)

Add the cloves and bayleaf, stir, then add the rest of the vegetables (except the beetroot, if you are using it). Stir well to mix the vegetables and spices, add the tomatoes with their juice and about 3 fl. oz (90 ml) water.

Cover and simmer over a gentle heat until the vegetables are softened (30 minutes approx.). Check from time to time, stir, and add a little more water if necessary. When the vegetables are tender add the beetroot, the desiccated coconut and a further 2 fl. oz (60 ml) water. Stir and leave over a lowish heat for about 5 minutes. Sprinkle with chopped fresh coriander and serve immediately with rice and mango chutney.

DIGESTION

Mr — , who loved buttered muffins but durst not eat them because they disagreed with his stomach, resolved to shoot himself; and then he eat three buttered muffins for breakfast before shooting himself, knowing that he should not be troubled with indigestion.

JAMES BOSWELL, 1740–95

I hope death will strike me
In the middle of a great meal
That I may be buried under the tablecloth
Between four ample dishes,
And on my tombstone will be written
This short inscription:
Here lies the first poet
Ever to die of indigestion.

MARC-ANTOINE DÉSAUGIERS, 1772–1827

Digestion, is the affair of the stomach: indigestion, that of the doctor; and the cure, that of chance.

LAUNCELOT STURGEON, *ESSAYS, MORAL, PHILOSOPHICAL, AND
STOMACHICAL, ON THE IMPORTANT SCIENCE OF GOOD-LIVING*, 1822

Of all corporeal operations, digestion is the one which has the most powerful influence on the mental state of the individual.

Nobody should be surprised by this assertion, for it could not be otherwise.

The most elementary rules of psychology teach us that the mind can only be impressed by means of its subject organs, which keep it in touch with external things; whence it follows that, when those organs are in poor condition, weak or inflamed, the deterioration inevitably influences the sensations, which are the intermediary and occasional means of intellectual activity.

Thus our accustomed manner of digesting, and particularly the latter part of the process, makes us habitually sad or gay, silent or talkative, morose or melancholy, without our being aware of it, and above all without being able to avoid it.

In this respect it would be possible to separate the civilized portion of mankind into three divisions, namely, the regular, the constipated, and the lax.

ANTHELME BRILLAT-SAVARIN, *PHYSIOLOGIE DU GOÛT*, 1825

No side dishes – no liqueurs. Only 2 or 3 wines. Whatever your stomach fancies – give it… Breakfast – fried ham and eggs, brown bread and a walk. Luncheon – a roast pigeon and fried potatoes, then a ride. Dinner at six, *not later, mind*; gravy soup, glass of sherry, nice fresh turbot and lobster sauce – wouldn't recommend salmon – another glass of sherry – then a good cut of the middle of a well-browned saddle of mutton, wash it over with a few glasses of iced champagne; and if you like a little light pastry to end up with, well and good. A pint of old port and a devilled biscuit can hurt no man. Mind, no salads or cucumbers or celery, at dinner, or fruit after. Turtle soup is very wholesome, so is venison. Don't let the punch be too acid, though.

R. S. SURTEES, *HANDLEY CROSS*, 1843

We live, not by what we eat but by what we digest; and what one man may digest, another would die of attempting. Rules on this subject are almost useless. Each man may soon learn the powers of his stomach, in health or disease, in this respect; and this ascertained, he has no more business to bring on indigestion than he has to get intoxicated or fall into debt. He who offends on these three points, deserves to forfeit stomach, head, and his electoral franchise.

DR JOHN DORAN, *TABLE TRAITS*, 1854

Adam and Eve were in Paradise. Why? Their digestion was good. Ah! then they took liberties, ate bad fruit, things they could not digest… Ah, to digest is to be happy.

ANTHONY TROLLOPE, *THE CLAVERINGS*, 1867

It is very strange, this domination of our intellect by our digestive organs. We cannot work, we cannot think, unless our stomach wills so. It dictates to us our emotions, our passions. After eggs and bacon, it says: 'Work!' After beefsteak and porter, it says: 'Sleep!' After a cup of tea (two spoonfuls for each cup, and don't let it stand more than three minutes), it says to the brain: 'Now, rise, and show your strength. Be eloquent, and deep, and tender; see, with a clear eye, into Nature and into life; spread your white wings of quivering thought, and soar, a godlike spirit, over the whirling world beneath you, up through long lanes of flaming stars to the gates of eternity!'

After hot muffins, it says: 'Be dull and soulless, like a beast of the field – a brain-

less animal with a listless eye, unlit by any ray of fancy, or of hope, or fear, or love, or life.' And after brandy, taken in sufficient quantity, it says: 'Now, come, fool, grin and tumble, that your fellow-men may laugh – drivel in folly, and splutter in senseless sounds, and show what a helpless ninny is poor man whose wit and will are drowned, like kittens, side by side, in half an inch of alcohol.'

We are but the veriest, sorriest slaves of our stomach. Reach not after morality and righteousness, my friends; watch vigilantly your stomach, and diet it with care and judgement. Then virtue and contentment will come and reign within your heart, unsought by any effort of your own; and you will be a good citizen, a loving husband, and a tender father – a noble, pious man.

JEROME K. JEROME, *THREE MEN IN A BOAT*, 1889

Olive oil is the very soul of a salad, and far beyond this, for it is one of the finest natural foods and medicines bestowed upon man. Let us away with salines and the depressing salts and substitute olive oil, which not only lubricates, but feeds the nerves, stimulates a proper functioning of the liver, upon which the happiness of man depends, and benevolently protects the mucous membranes from the noxious effects of biting acids. True wisdom would cause dictators to administer olive, rather than castor, oil. And there is no need to cause the repulsion of a heavy dosage. A teaspoonful a day, taken with vegetables in the course of the daily meals, will calm the troubles of many a storm-tossed digestion, and make the world a better place for the brief dwelling of man.

EDWARD AND LORNA BUNYARD, *THE EPICURE'S COMPANION*, 1937

DINING

When you with Hoch Dutch Heeren dine,
Expect false Latin and stummed wine:
They never taste who always drink,
They always talk, who never think,

MATTHEW PRIOR, 1664–1721

A man is in general better pleased when he has a good dinner upon his table than when his wife talks Greek.

DR JOHNSON IN JAMES BOSWELL, *LIFE OF SAMUEL JOHNSON*, 1791

Despite two hundred years of supposed progress I suspect Dr Johnson's observation still applies, though few dare admit it. The only difference at the end of the twentieth century is that we men have to pretend we prefer our wives to master Ancient Greek... but hope they manage to conjure up something rather tasty as well. Annie says the difference for women is that they now feel they have to be able to do both. That's progress for you!

I am fond of a good dinner, and many of my luckiest thoughts have occurred to me while handling – not the pen, but the knife and fork.

LORD BYRON, 1788–1824

A true epicure would as soon fast as be obliged to hurry over a good dinner.

LAUNCELOT STURGEON, *ESSAYS, MORAL, PHILOSOPHICAL AND STOMACHICAL, ON THE IMPORTANCE OF GOOD-LIVING*, 1822

I consider five or even six o'clock, as too early for a man deeply engaged in business. By dining at seven or eight, one gains a whole hour or two of sobriety, for transacting the more serious affairs of life. In other words, no man can do anything but drink after dinner; and thus it follows that the later one dines, the less does one's drinking break in upon that valuable concern, time, of which, whatever may be the case with others, I, for one, have always had more of than of money. A man, however busy, who sits down to dinner as eight strikes, may say to himself with a placid conscience – Come, fairplay is a jewel - the day is over – nothing but boozing until bed-time.

WILLIAM MAGINN, *MAXIMS OF SIR WILLIAM O'DOHERTY, BART.*, 1849

Ladies, though they like good things at picnics, and indeed, at other times... very seldom prepare dainties for themselves alone. Men are wiser and more thoughtful, and are careful to have the good things, even if they are to be enjoyed without companionship.

ANTHONY TROLLOPE, *HE KNEW HE WAS RIGHT*, 1869

Sir, respect your dinner, idolize it, enjoy it properly. You will be by many hours in the week, many weeks in the year, and many years in your life, happier, if you do.

WILLIAM MAKEPEACE THACKERAY, *MEMORIALS OF GORMANDIZING*

One cannot think well, love well, sleep well, if one has not dined well.

VIRGINIA WOOLF, *A ROOM OF ONE'S OWN*, 1929

DINNER PARTIES

A round table, holding eight;
A hearty welcome and little state;
One dish set on a time,
As plain as you please, but always prime;
Beer for asking for – and in pewter;
Servants who don't require a tutor;
Talking guests and dumb-waiters;
Warm plates and hot potaters.

ANON

July 27, 1774

I breakfasted, dined, supped and slept again at College… Mr Hindley, Dr Thurlowe, Master of the Temple, Dr Burrows, Dr Birchenden, and Mr Bowerbank dined and spent the afternoon with me at New College. I borrowed the Chequer Room of the Bursars for my company to dine in. We were very merry and pushed the bottle briskly. I gave my com-

pany for dinner, some green Pea soup, a chine of Mutton, some New College Puddings, a goose, some Peas and a Codlin Tart with Cream. Madeira and Port Wine to drink after and at dinner some strong Beer, Cyder, Ale and small Beer. Dr West spent part of the afternoon and supped and spent the evening with me. I had a handsome dish of fruit after dinner. At 7 o'clock we all went from the Chequer to my Room where we had Coffee and Tea. Dr Birchenden went from us soon after coffee and did not return again… Mr Hindley, Dr Thurlowe, Dr West, Dr Burrows and Mr Bowerbank, supped and stayed with me till after one. Mr Hindley, Dr Burrows, Mr Bowerbank and myself got to cards after coffee. At whist I won 1.0.6 out of which, Mr Hindley owes me 0.5.0. I gave my company only for supper cold mutton. After supper I gave them to drink some Arrac Punch with Jellies in it and some Port wine. I made all my Company but Dr West quite merry. We drank 8 bottles of Port one Bottle of Madeira besides Arrac Punch, Beer and Cyder. I carried off my drinking exceedingly well indeed.

JAMES WOODFORDE, *THE DIARY OF A COUNTRY PARSON 1758–1781*

(ED. JOHN BERESFORD)

Sir, when a man is invited to dinner, he is disappointed if he does not get something good.

DR SAMUEL JOHNSON, 1709–84

His [Dr Johnson's] invitations to dinner abroad were numerous, and he seldom balked them. When invited to dine, even with an intimate friend, he was not pleased if something better than a plain dinner was not prepared for him. I have heard him say on such an occasion, 'This was a good dinner enough, to be sure: but it was not a dinner to *ask* a man to.' On the other hand he was wont to express, with great glee, his satisfaction when he had been entertained quite to his mind.

SIR JOHN HAWKINS, *THE LIFE AND WORKS OF SAMUEL JOHNSON*, 1787–9

It is contrary to every acknowledged principle of moral rectitude, to speak ill of the man at whose house you have dined – *during a space of time proportioned to the excellence of the fare.* For an ordinary dinner a week is generally sufficient; and it can, in no case, exceed a month; at the expiration of which time the tongue is once more at liberty.

LAUNCELOT STURGEON, *ESSAYS, MORAL, PHILOSOPHICAL AND STOMACHICAL, ON THE IMPORTANT SCIENCE OF GOOD-LIVING*, 1822

In England Dinner-giving Snobs occupy a very important place in society, and the task of describing them is tremendous. There was a time in my life when the consciousness of having eaten a man's salt rendered me dumb regarding his demerits, and I thought it a wicked act and a breach of hospitality to speak ill of him.

But why should a saddle-of-mutton blind you, or a turbot and lobster-sauce shut your mouth for ever? With advancing age men see their duties more clearly. I am not to be hoodwinked any longer by a slice of venison, be it ever so fat; and as for being dumb on account of turbot and lobster-sauce – of course I am; good manners ordain that I should be so, until I have swallowed the compound – but not afterwards; directly the victuals are discussed, and John takes away the plate, my tongue begins to wag…

'What *is* a Dinner-giving Snob?' some innocent youth, who is not *répandu* in the world may ask – or some simple reader who has not the benefits of London experience.

My dear sir, I will show you – not all, for that is impossible – but several kinds of Dinner-giving Snobs. For instance, suppose you, in the middle rank of life, accustomed to Mutton, roast on Tuesday, cold on Wednesday, hashed on Thursday &c., with small means and a small establishment, choose to waste the former and set the latter topsy-turvy by giving entertainments unnaturally costly – you come into the Dinner-giving Snob class at once… Suppose you pretend to be richer and grander than you ought to be – you are a Dinner-giving Snob…

A man who goes out of his natural sphere of society to ask Lords, Generals, Aldermen, and other persons of fashion, but is niggardly of his hospitality towards his own equals, is a Dinner-giving Snob… Stinginess is snobbish. Ostentation is snobbish. Too great profusion is snobbish. Tuft-hunting is snobbish. But I own there are people more snobbish than all those whose defects are above-mentioned: viz., those individuals who can, and don't give dinners at all.

WILLIAM MAKEPEACE THACKERAY, *THE BOOK OF SNOBS*, 1848

Most London dinners evaporate in whispers to one's next door neighbour. I make it a rule never to speak a word to mine, but fire across the table; though I broke it once when I heard a lady who sat next me, in a low, sweet voice, say, 'No gravy, sir.' I had never seen her before, but I turned suddenly round and said, 'Madam, I have been looking for a person who disliked gravy all my life; let us swear eternal friendship.' She looked astonished, but took the oath, and, what is better, kept it.

SYDNEY SMITH IN *A MEMOIR OF THE REVD SYDNEY SMITH* BY
LADY HOLLAND, 1855

Let the number of guests be no more than twelve, chosen for the variety of their occupations but the similarity of their tastes; let the dining room be brilliantly lit, the cloth pure white, the temperature between 60 and 68 degrees; let the men be witty and not pedantic, the women amiable but not too coquettish; let the dishes be few in number but exquisite, the wines vintage… ; eating should be unhurried, for dinner is the final business of the day; the coffee should be hot… ; let the drawing room be large enough so that those who wish may play cards while leaving room for after-dinner conversation… ; the tea should not be too strong, the toast should be artistically buttered… ; the signal to leave should not come before eleven and everyone should be in bed by midnight.

ANTHELME BRILLAT-SAVARIN, *PHYSIOLOGIE DU GOÛT*, 1825

———

DINNER PARTIES. – As we have before observed, 'Man is a dining animal,' and we contend that young people as well as old can really enjoy a dinner party, and that everyone can appreciate a good one – only they involve a greater amount of thought than many are prepared to bestow.

Let no one imagine that to give wines and meats of the best and most costly kind, is to ensure one's guests' enjoyment of the same, for there are few of us whose painful experience it has not been to sigh over a dinner, which in itself was irreproachable and which might have been enjoyable, but – was quite the contrary.

There are many more things to be considered than the actual dinner itself, if one aspires to be a successful dinner giver, but there is one golden rule which, if everyone observed, would at any rate prevent many failures and that is our advice to all who entertain, 'Keep within your means.'

We mean this in the broadest sense not simply to spend more than one can afford, for many can spare money who cannot give time, and many more can do the former, who have not the room, convenience, or faculty, for entertainment.

Dinners, like dresses, want consideration; a picnic may be impromptu, in fact those hastily arranged are very often the most enjoyable, but there is not, or ought not to be (unless for a small unceremonious one), anything impromptu about a dinner.

What we wish to imply by keeping within one's means is not to entertain to the limit of our resources, and we hope our readers will not consider us impertinent in giving them the following advice:–

NUMBER OF GUESTS. – Never ask more people than you can comfortably seat, or than you have servants to wait upon. Think well over your list of guests before you invite them, and plan how you can arrange them at table, so that you can feel beforehand that you can give each guest a companion who will in all probability be a pleasant one, which, if it be a large party will greatly lessen your responsibilities.

DINNER GIVING. – The next thing to be thought of is the dinner, and varying that very good old maxim, 'Cut your cloak according to your cloth,' we should say, choose your dinner according to your cook. When fortunate enough to possess a thoroughly good one, one need not be afraid of trying a few experiments, but otherwise it is a dangerous thing, and if any contretemps occur, it is the mistress, and not the cook, who suffers.

It is a grand thing to feel confident of what is coming to table, when one is at the head of it, and no hostess is likely to be quite happy or at ease with any fear on her mind as to how the next course will turn out.

TEMPERATURE OF ROOM. – Another very important thing very often overlooked, is the temperature of the dining room... We maintain that it is not possible to thoroughly enjoy a good dinner in a room either too hot or too cold, and would ask hostesses to well consider the subject.

LIGHTING. – Next we come to the lighting of the room, by no means a small matter... The thing to be arrived at for comfort and effect is that a pleasant and sufficient light be thrown from above, and concentrated upon the table and guests, whilst the remainder of the room may be in *comparative* shadow, with only enough light for the servants to do their work.

MRS BEETON, *MRS BEETON'S BOOK OF HOUSEHOLD MANAGEMENT*, 1861

How very right Mrs Beeton and Brillat-Savarin are on the question of room temperature. I've known many a good dinner blighted by a howling draught or a roaring fire inches from the back of the chair. When the room is uncomfortable the most delicious food can lose a lot of its savour. Perhaps that's why so many of the most memorable dinners are the ones eaten in the informal cosiness of a friend's kitchen. We owe this pleasure to the more relaxed rules of modern entertaining. What a contrast between suppers in the kitchen and the formality described by E. F. Benson, author of those wonderful *Mapp and Lucia* stories, in this sketch of a typical dinner party given by his father, the Archbishop of Canterbury, in the 1870s.

We were ready, on the first sound of the front-door bell, breathlessly to watch from the passage that ran round the hall the arrival of the splendid guests. The men put down their hats and coats in the outer hall (of which through the banisters, but not over them, I commanded an admirable view) and waited for the emergence of their ladies from my mother's sitting-room, where the workboxes and lazy-tongs had been put away and pins and brushes and looking-glasses provided for their titivation.

They had gone in mere chrysalides, swathed in shawls and plaids; they emerged magnificent butterflies, all green and pink and purple. As each came floating forth, her husband offered her his arm, and they went thus into the drawing-room. When all were assembled, the gong boomed, and out they came again, having changed partners, and the galaxy passed into the glittering cave of Aladdin next door. Grace was said, and they sat down to the incredible banquet.

There was thick soup and clear soup (a nimble gourmand had been known to secure both). Clear soup in those days had a good deal of sherry in it. There was a great boiled turbot with his head lolling over one end of the dish, and his tail over the other: then came a short pause, while at the four corners of the table were placed the four entrées. Two were brown entrées, made of beef, mutton, or venison; two were white entrées, made of chicken, brains, rabbit, or sweetbreads, and these were handed round in pairs. ('Brown or white, madam?')

Then came a joint made of the brown meat which had not figured in the brown entrées, or if only beef and mutton were in season, the joint might be a boiled ham. My mother always carved this herself instead of my father: this was rather daring, rather modern, but she carved with swift artistic skill and he did not, and she invariably refused the offer of her neighbouring gentleman to relieve her of the task.

Then came a dish of birds, duck or game, and a choice followed between substantial puddings and more airy confections covered with blobs of cream and jewels of angelica and ornamental sugarings. A stilton cheese succeeded and then dessert. My mother collected the ladies' eyes, and the ladies collected their fans and scent-bottles and scarves, and left the gentlemen to their wine...

In these festive evenings of the seventies, prolonged drinking of port and claret had gone out, smoking had not yet come in, and so, when the decanters of port and claret had gone round twice, and sherry had been offered (it was called a white-wash), the host rang the bell for coffee. The men then joined the ladies, and the ladies, who had been chattering together in a bunch, swiftly broke up, like scattered globules of quicksilver, so that next each of them should be a vacant chair, into which a man inserted himself, prudently avoiding those who had been his neighbours at dinner. A number of conversational duets then took place, but these did not last long, for there was certain to be a lady present who sang very sweetly.

E. F. Benson, *As We Were*, 1930

It is very poor consolation to be told that the man who has given one a bad dinner, or poor wine, is irreproachable in private life. Even the cardinal virtues cannot atone for half-cold entrées.

Oscar Wilde, *The Picture of Dorian Gray*, 1891

A man who can dominate a London dinner-table can dominate the world.

Oscar Wilde, *A Woman of No Importance*, 1893

Dinner at Blenheim Palace

We had a good chef, but there had to be perfect co-operation with the butler in order to serve an eight-course dinner within the hour we had prescribed as the time limit. This was not an easy matter, since the kitchen was at least three hundred yards from the dining room. We had imposed this limit to prevent the prolonged delays that occur between courses. It also appeared to us sufficient time to linger over dinner, since the men spent an additonal half-hour over coffee and liqueurs. But such a schedule had at times its draw-backs, and at Lady Londonderry's, where the rule was most rigorously enforced, I once watched with amusement the silent but no less furious battle between a reputed gourmet who wished to eat every morsel of his large helping and a footman equally determined to remove his plate...

Two soups, one hot and one cold, were served simultaneously. Then came two fish, again one hot and one cold, with accompanying sauces. I still remember my intense annoyance with a very greedy man who complained bitterly that both his favourite fish were being served and that he wished to eat both, so that I had to keep the service waiting while he consumed first the hot and then the cold, quite unperturbed at the delay he was causing. An entrée was succeeded by a meat dish. Sometimes a sorbet preceded the game, which in the shooting season was varied, comprising grouse, partridge, pheasant, duck, woodcock and snipe. In the summer, when there was no game, we had quails from Egypt, fattened in Europe, and ortolans from France, which cost a fortune. An elaborate sweet followed, succeeded by a hot savoury with which was drunk the port so comforting to English palates. The dinner ended with a succulent array of peaches, plums, apricots, nectarines, strawberries, raspberries, pears and grapes, all grouped in generous pyramids among the flowers that adorned the table.

At the end of the prescribed hour I rose to lead the ladies to the Long Library, where Mr Perkins, an organist of repute, was playing Bach or Wagner. If our guests were younger, an Austrian orchestra summoned from London played the Viennese waltzes which were then the rage.

CONSUELO VANDERBILT BALSAN (DUCHESS OF MARLBOROUGH),
THE GLITTER AND THE GOLD, 1953

Matters of taste must be felt, not dogmatized about. A large crayfish of lobster rearing itself menacingly on its tail seems quite at home on the sideboard of a Brighton Hotel-de-luxe, but will intimidate a shy guest at a small dinner party.

LADY JEKYLL, *KITCHEN ESSAYS*, 1922

At a dinner party one should eat wisely but not too well, and talk well, but not too wisely.

W. SOMERSET MAUGHAM, 1874–1965

After all the thought, effort, time, money and energy put into your dinner party you can only hope that your guests do not depart into the night muttering, along with a disgruntled Dr Johnson: 'This was a good dinner enough, to be sure: but it was not a dinner to *ask* a man to.'

DRINKING

Happy the natives of Bordeaux, for whom living and drinking are one and the same thing.

AUSONIUS, C. 309–92

This section praises the art of drinking, and quite right too. But before going ahead and drawing your attention to the pleasures of the grape and the hop, I feel a duty to make a passing mention of The Hangover.

'Why, oh why, oh why,' teetotallers cry, 'do people have to drink at all?' 'Because', the drinkers reply, 'we feel so good while we are doing it.' 'Ah, yes,' say the sober and righteous ones, 'but what of the dreaded aftermath, the hangover?' As there is no real answer to this, the topers can only resort to mocking these Puritans in the words of the late, great comedian W. C. Fields: 'Teetotallers – I pity them. Fancy waking up in the morning and knowing that's as good as you're going to feel all day!'

To alleviate a hangover many people advise drinking a pint of water immediately after an evening's boozing. The problem with this is that one can have difficulty finding the sink, let alone filling a glass with a pint of water. No, you will have to suffer for your weakness of character and drink several pints of God's own liquid (Château la Pompe as I have heard it rather fetchingly called) the following day. This eventually cures the dehydration, the cause of your misery.

Another supposed cure is to take a nip the next morning of whatever it was you were drinking the night before. For the uninitiated this is called 'the hair of the dog' and is decidedly *not* recommended as in my experience it provokes an appetite for carrying on with the supposed cure for the rest of the day on into the evening, by which time you're right back where you started.

Drinking is undoubtedly one of the great solaces of life. To prevent it becoming a treacherous pastime it's best to heed the profound phrase 'know thyself'. A friend of mine, on reaching the age of sixty, told me sadly, 'I've had to give it all up – with me it's either no drinks, or nine.' Sad indeed, but the only solution if you can't take it, or – more importantly – if your family can't take you taking it.

This reminds me of the drinking careers of some of my ancestors. My great-grandfather was known as a 'two-bottle man'. In those distant days that meant he could consume two bottles of port before lunch. Incredible! But they built them tough in those days. Great-grandad eventually built himself up to nearly twenty-three stone, and still appeared to enjoy life and his extraordinary diet, until one day he fell right through the floor of his carriage. The result was not fatal but encouraged him to slim down a bit.

My grandfather was a one-and-a-half-bottle man (mainly whisky) and lived well into his seventies. When he expired the doctors asked if they could carry out an autopsy because they couldn't believe he had reached such a good age with lifetime habits like his. The family was just as curious, and in due course the medics opened the old boy up and were fairly astounded to find no trace of a liver at all!

My father attempted to emulate his impressive predecessors but wasn't up to it, and finished up consuming a mere half a bottle of sherry a day. His son likes to think he is made of the same stout stuff as his forebears, but having been an actor for most of his adult life he does not take a sip until the curtain has fallen, by which time, fortunately, it's too late to do a lot of damage.

To Celia

Drink to me only with thine eyes,
And I will pledge with mine;
Or leave a kiss but in the cup
And I'll not look for wine.
The thirst that from the soul doth rise
Doth ask a drink divine;
But might I of Jove's nectar sup,
I would not change for thine.

BEN JONSON, 1572–1637

Drunkeness

Some men are drunke, and being drunke will fight;
Some men are drunke and being drunke are merrie;
Some men are drunke, and secrets bring to light;
Some men are drunke and being drunke are sorie:
Thus may we see that drunken men haue passions,
And drunkeness hath many foolish fashions.

Fishes that in the sea do drinke their fill,
Teach men by nature to shun drunkenesse.
What bird is there, that with his chirping bill
Of any liquor ever tooke excesse?
Thus beastes on earth, fish in seas, birds in skie,
Teach men to shun all superfluitie.

Would any heare the discommodities
That doe arise from our excess of drinke?
It duls the braine, it hurts the memorie,
It blinds the sight, it makes men bleare-eyd blinke;
It kils the bodie, and it wounds the soule;
Leaue, therefore, leaue, O leaue this vice so foul!

JOHN LANE, *FL.* 1621

If you intend to drink much *after* dinner, never drink much *at* dinner, and particularly avoid mixing wines. If you begin with Sauterne, for example, stick to the Sauterne, though, on the whole, red wines are best. Avoid malt liquor most cautiously; for nothing is so apt to get into the head unawares, or, what is almost as bad, to fill the stomach with wind. Champagne, on the latter account, is bad. Port, three glasses at dinner – claret, three bottles after: behold the fair proportion, and the most excellent wines.

WILLIAM MAGINN, *MAXIMS OF SIR WILLIAM O'DOHERTY, BART.*, 1849

I went to Frankfort and got drunk
With that most learn'd professor, Brunck;
I went to Wortz and got more drunken
With that more learn'd professor, Ruhnken.

RICHARD PORSON, *PORSONIANA*, 1856

Ah, fill the cup: – what boots it to repeat
How time is slipping underneath our Feet:
Unborn Tomorrow and dead Yesterday,
Why fret about them if Today be sweet!

EDWARD FITZGERALD, *THE RUBÁIYÁT OF OMAR KHAYYÁM*, 1859

Here's to a temperance supper,
With water in glasses tall,
And coffee and tea to end with –
And me not there at all!

ANON

Then as to feasting, it doesn't agree with me –
Each single goblet is equal to three with me,
Wine is my foe, tho' I still am a friend of it,
Hock becomes hic – with a cup at the end of it!

OLIVER WENDELL HOLMES, 1809–94

I have made an important discovery… that alcohol, taken in sufficient
quantities, produces all the effects of intoxication.

OSCAR WILDE

THE LOGICAL VEGETARIAN

You will find me drinking rum,
Like a sailor in a slum,
You will find me drinking beer like a Bavarian,
You will find me drinking gin
In the lowest kind of inn,
Because I am a rigid Vegetarian.
No more the milk of cows
Shall pollute my private house
Than the milk of the wild mares of the Barbarian;
I will stick to port and sherry,
For they are so very, very,
So very, very, very Vegetarian.

G. K. CHESTERTON, 1874–1936

There are several reasons for drinking,
And one has just entered my head;
If a man cannot drink when he's living
How the Hell can he drink when he's dead?

ANON

A Prohibitionist is the sort of man one wouldn't care to drink with – even if he drank.

H. L. MENCKEN

Late, late in the night we recalled that Horace says fried shrimps and African snails will cure a hangover. None was available... we tore the remedy down to its fundamentals and decided that it was a good strong dose of proteins and alcohol, so we substituted a new compound – fried fish and a dash of medicinal whisky, and it did the job.

JOHN STEINBECK, 29 MARCH 1940

The British habit of drinking whilst standing up is barbaric.

GLANVIL HALL (ATTRIBUTED)

Eating Alone

Eating alone is a common experience for actors after a performance, particularly in strange places while on tour. Sometimes it can be quite a relief, after being so closely involved with a small group of people, to get back to your hotel room or little flat and have a nice quiet meal. Sometimes it's simply because you don't feel brave enough to sit all alone in a restaurant, with or without the comfort and companionship of a good book. I recently read an account of an interview with fellow thespian Robert Powell, who recounted how he ate by himself in his room each night for several months while filming in France, because he felt selfconscious being alone in the hotel restaurant. Perhaps he had once suffered an experience similar to the one so feelingly described here.

If I were the head-waiter of a smart new restaurant I should call my under-waiters together on the afternoon of the opening night and say to them, 'George, Alphonse, Henri! Remember this. To make much of the solitary diner. Serve him first. Ply him with surreptitious rolls. And let the wine-list, open at page six, be promptly at his elbow. I do not want to hear the phrase "In one moment, sir," addressed in this establishment to any party of less than two.'

On page six of the wine-list are of course the clarets.

No such instructions have ever been given to the waiters at any restaurant at which I have dined alone. 'Solitary gentlemen', the head-waiter has ordered, 'may be disregarded. Our covers have not been spread for the benefit of persons with evening papers jammed into their jacket pockets. Make them feel their position. Set them, if you can, immediately adjacent to the service door, but facing the room, so that they may have the humiliation of raising a hand at you every time you flash by into the kitchen. You will find it convenient, too, to have the unoccupied end of their table to rest your trays on when you wish to alter the balance or to scribble a note on your pads. But there must be no open rudeness. When you whip the menu-card from beneath their noses to present it to a party of four who have just come in a murmured apology is in order. Nor should you fail to return the card when the new party have been served. One of your colleagues may need it elsewhere in the room.'

I think the psychology behind the head-waiter's instructions is wrong. As an immediate financial proposition the solitary diner is not, I grant him, to be compared with the party of four. Alone, a man who catches sight of the prices on page six is at liberty to turn with a shudder to the end of the book and order a lager. But in company, conscious of three pairs of eyes so studiously averted, the same man has no option. He may shudder, but, if only to break the unendurable silence, he must plump for No. 62 at forty-eight and sixpence. To watch the air of studied unconcern with which such a man returns the wine-list to the waiter and turns brightly to the lady on his left is one of the solitary diner's few consolations for his state. But let the head-waiter remember that the lone wolf of to-day may be the genial host of to-morrow. He may return, for all the head-waiter knows, at the head of a party of twelve. He may even recommend it to someone who puts his expenses down to the firm.

And your solitary diner sees everything. He is of all men the most observant, the most sensitive, the most ready to take offence. To the party of four at the next table, with their gay talk, their bursts of laughter, their quick turns of the head and whispered sallies at his expense, the minutes that elapse before the arrival of the soup may pass unnoticed. You will see them sometimes with their heads so close together that the waiter must cough and make a little clatter with his tray before he can manoeuvre their plates into position. Not so the solitary man. The passage of time is not likely to catch *him* unawares. He wants something to do with his hands, and he wants it badly... If he can't have a roll to crumble, then in Heaven's name let him have a soup-plate to bend his reddening face above.

To a man in such a state as this five minutes are five minutes and ten minutes are a lifetime. I do not believe that the waiter who finally comes to rest at his elbow and says brightly, 'Now, sir!' is handling him in the best possible way. Nor, in my opinion, should any waiter, after taking his order, add casually, 'And a lager to go with it, sir?' When my financial standing is summed up in this contemptuous way I abandon my intention of having

a lager without hesitation and abruptly demand to see the wine-list. When it comes I turn at once to page six and order a bottle of No. 70, which as everyone knows, is priced at sixty-three shillings. This puts the man in his place and ensures that by the time I come to pay the bill I am sitting sideways at the table, with my legs crossed, and looking quite boldly about the room again. I may even be swishing the remains of the claret about in my glass in an off-hand sort of way. I then give the waiter a thundering tip to complete his discomfiture and sweep out.

But I never go back there – at least, not with a party. I wouldn't take people to such a place.

H. F. ELLIS, *PUNCH MAGAZINE*, SEPTEMBER 1947

———

Of course, eating after the show does not always mean eating alone. Far from it, in fact. Many of the best times are the meals shared when the curtain comes down and we are all too high on adrenalin to go straight home to bed. At other times you long for a quiet supper at home, particularly when you are married to someone in the business, who understands the need for a wind-down at the end of the evening.

Athene Seyler, the great comedy actress, and her beloved husband, Nicholas (Beau) Hannen, often worked together in the West End theatre. Athene used to say that, always in a rush to get home to their flat in Hammersmith after the show, from hunger and absentmindedness they often forgot to take off their hats before they started cooking their supper. Sir John Gielgud is reputed to have remarked, 'Did you know, Athene and Beau always cook in their hats? Extraordinary! Enhances the flavour I suppose.'

Another great theatrical couple, Dame Sybil Thorndike and Sir Lewis Casson, were contemporaries of Athene. I was lucky enough to work with all three of them in a West End revival of *Arsenic and Old Lace* in 1966. Dame Sybil was *not* a great one for cooking, and once said that their favourite late-night snack was marmalade sandwiches with cocoa.

In 1952 many well-known members of the theatrical profession contributed to a book of recipes in aid of the Actors' Orphanage and, despite her self-confessed lack of culinary skill, Dame Sybil made a characteristic contribution. Here it is:

STEW

I'm no cook, I make stews and porridge; and the usual everyday stew is the thing I suppose. Here goes.

Take anything that's left over, fry it all up with more vegetables of any or every sort. Put any flavouring you like (Worcester sauce by me preferred) cook and cook and cook and cook, till it's a gorgeous mess. And if you don't like it I've no use for you at all: for it's lovely.

————

Recipes suitable for after-show eating tend to divide between those that can be left cooking slowly for hours, and those that can be prepared quickly – perhaps while drinking a welcome glass of wine – and consumed immediately. I have found that dishes such as stews, casseroles, fish pie and shepherd's pie are good, as they can cook quietly for a long time and people can take what they want then put the dish back in the oven – useful if there are other members of the family to be catered for as well as the actors.

Another standby is The Quiche. Once when we were staying with a dear friend, Hilary Bell, who has a low opinion of her own cooking, she brought a dish to the table announcing cheerfully, 'This is my Quiche of Death.' It's true quiches can be awful – soggy and tasteless or dry and boring – though hers wasn't! But they *can* be both delicious and useful, as they can be eaten hot, with vegetables, by the family, then later eaten cold, with some salad, by the 'evening worker'. 'Quiche of Death' has become a family saying but Richard has suggested that I should call my recipe 'Quiche of Life': I hope that won't seem big-headed!

QUICHE OF LIFE
I concocted this recipe because I had a lot of ham left one Christmas, but you could use less ham and a greater variety of vegetables. It serves 4.

Make shortcrust pastry in your usual way, using 8 oz (225 g) plain flour. Put the dough in a plastic bag and leave to rest in the fridge for about 30 minutes.
8 oz (225 g) ham, diced
4 oz (110 g) mushrooms, sliced
½ sweet red pepper, diced
4 oz (110 g) cheese (Gruyère is particularly good), grated
2 eggs
¼ pint (150 ml) cream and plain yoghurt mixed together
1 tablespoon fresh herbs, finely chopped
salt and pepper to taste
½ teaspoon paprika (optional)

Sauté the vegetables quickly, taking care not to let the juice begin to come out of the mushrooms (you may need to add these to the pan last). Mix with the diced ham and add the herbs. (I used fresh sage and rosemary left over from Christmas; they worked well but it's a matter of choice and what is going into the filling.)

Roll out the pastry, quite thinly, and line a very lightly greased flan dish. Spread the ham and vegetable mixture over the pastry base.

Lightly beat the eggs and add to the cream and yoghurt mixture. Add 3 oz (75 g) of the grated cheese and some freshly ground pepper and salt, depending on the saltiness of the ham. Mix well and spoon over the ham and vegetable mixture, spreading evenly.

Sprinkle the remaining cheese over the top and place in the centre of a preheated oven at approximately 200°C (400°F) gas mark 6. After 10 minutes reduce the heat to about 180°C (350°F) gas mark 4 for another 10 minutes until the pastry is cooked through and the egg mixture is set and golden on top.

ETIQUETTE

TABLE MANNERS FOR CHILDREN

When ye be set, keep your own knife clean and sharp, that so ye may carve honestly your own meat.

Let courtesy and silence dwell with you, and tell no foul tales to another.

Cut your bread with your knife and break it not. Lay a clean trencher before you, and when the potage is brought, take your spoon and eat quietly; and do not leave the spoon in the dish I pray you.

Look ye be not caught leaning on the table, and keep clear of soiling the cloth.

Do not hang your head over your dish, or in any wise drink with full mouth.

Keep from picking your nose, your teeth, your nails, at meal time – so we are taught.

Advise you against taking so muckle meat into your mouth but that ye may right well answer when men speak to you.

When ye shall drink, wipe your mouth clean with a cloth, and your hands also, so that you shall not in any way soil the cup, for then shall none of your companions be loth to drink with you.

Likewise, do not touch the salt in the salt-cellar with any meat; but lay salt honestly on your trencher, for that is courtesy.

Do not carry your knife to your mouth with food, or hold the meat with your hands in any wise; and also if divers good means are brought to you, look that with courtesy ye assay of each; and if your dish be taken away with its meat and another brought, courtesy demands that ye shall let it go, and not ask for it back again.

And if strangers be set at table with you, and savoury meat be brought or sent to you, make them good cheer with part of it, for certainly it is not polite when others be present at meat with you, to keep all that is brought you, and like churls vouchsafe nothing to others.

Do not cut your meat like field-men who have such an appetite that they reck not in what wise, where or when or how ungodly they hack at their meat; but, sweet children, have always your delight in courtesy and in gentleness, and eschew boisterousness with all your might.

The Babees' Book, c. 1475

Being set at the table, scratch not thyself, and take thou heed as much as thou can'st to spit, cough and blow at thy nose; but if it be needful, do it dexterously without much noise, turning thy face sideling.

FRANCES HAWKINS, *YOUTH'S BEHAVIOUR*, 1663

To commence with your entrance into the drawing room – don't stand bowing at the door, as if you had a petition to present; but stride confidently up to the lady of the house, and so close before you make your obeisance, that you nearly thrust your head into her face.

When dinner is announced – if you should follow a lady to the dining room, don't tread upon her train, nor step back, to avoid it, upon the toes of her behind you; and if it should be your lot to hand one to her seat – endeavour to avoid tumbling over the chairs in your hurry to place her...

Whatever may be your inclination, cautiously abstain from being helped a second time from the same dish: a man's character has been damned in society in consequence of being stigmatized as '*one of those fellows who call twice for soup!*'

LAUNCELOT STURGEON, *ESSAYS, MORAL, PHILOSOPHICAL AND STOMACHICAL, ON THE IMPORTANT SCIENCE OF GOOD-LIVING*, 1822

In helping a lady to wine, *always* fill the glass to the very brim, for custom prevents them from taking many glasses at a time; and I have seen cross looks when the rule has been neglected by young and inexperienced dandies.

WILLIAM MAGINN, *MAXIMS OF SIR WILLIAM O'DOHERTY, BART.*, 1849

We could not lead a pleasant life,
And t'would be finished soon,
If peas were eaten with the knife,
And gravy with the spoon.

Eat slowly: only men in rags
And gluttons old in sin
Mistake themselves for carpet bags
And tumble victuals in.

SIR WALTER ALEXANDER RALEIGH, *LAUGHTER FROM A CLOUD*, 1923

The tale goes that an irate Colonel, who had just heard where his place was to be at the dinner table, said to his charming hostess that, 'Of course it was a matter of no importance, but he thought in his position he really ought to tell her he was a full Colonel.' She only said, 'Are you really? Well I hope that when dinner is over you will be still fuller.'

LADY WILSON, *LETTERS FROM INDIA*

To be enjoyed thoroughly an apple must be eaten lustily and without manners.

RICHARDSON WRIGHT, *THE BED-BOOK OF EATING AND DRINKING*, 1943

The three great stumbling-blocks in a girl's education, she says, are *homard à l'Américaine*, a boiled egg, and asparagus. Shoddy table manners, she says, have broken up many a happy home.

COLETTE, *GIGI*, 1945

I eat my peas with honey
I've done it all my life
It makes the peas taste funny
But it keeps 'em on the knife!

ANON

HOW TO GET ON IN SOCIETY

Phone for the fish-knives, Norman
As cook is a little unnerved;
You kiddies have crumpled the serviettes
And I must have things daintily served.

Are the requisites all in the toilet?
The frills round the cutlets can wait
Till the girl has replenished the cruets
And switched on the logs in the grate.

It's ever so close in the lounge, dear,
But the vestibule's comfy for tea
And Howard is out riding on horseback,
So do come and take some with me.

Now here is a fork for your pastries,
And do use the couch for your feet;
I know what I wanted to ask you –
Is trifle sufficient for sweet?

Milk and then just as it comes dear?
I'm afraid the preserve's full of stones;
Beg pardon, I'm soiling the doileys
With afternoon tea-cakes and scones.

JOHN BETJEMAN

FISH

There is an apocryphal story, with a strong ring of truth to it, that we always think of when fish is on the menu. A penniless actor cannot afford to pay his train fare to a job with a repertory theatre in one of the further-flung corners of the British Isles. Ingenuity and determination come to the rescue and he manages to cadge a ride – a rather slow ride – on a barge transporting a load of fish up north. As the barge is tied up at its destination someone calls out, 'Ahoy there! What's your cargo?'

'Fish and actors,' shouts back the bargee.

To which the actor responds indignantly, 'I'm *very* concerned about the billing.'

It is therefore quite appropriate that this fish pie, which is a favourite in our house, is based on a recipe of that most eminent actor, Sir Ian McKellen. In his instructions Sir Ian says that his recipe serves '4–6 ordinary people or 2 hungry actors'! It is a reminder that actors are renowned for demolishing any decent food that is put in their way – either because they are 'resting' and in need of a square meal, or because they are working, so they come off stage ravenously hungry. We have a theory that it is an inherited characteristic, stemming from the days when actors were strolling players, who never quite knew where the next meal was coming from. No wonder Shakespeare, an actor who knew the realities of the profession, made Hamlet say to Polonius: 'Good my lord, will you see the players well bestowed? Do you hear, let them be well used.'

In 1990 we went on a world tour with the Renaissance Theatre Company, performing in *King Lear* and *A Midsummer Night's Dream*. In Budapest we were invited to a party given by Julian and Guinevere Harvey, who worked for the British Council. After all the official stand-up bashes we had been to, it was wonderful to be in a lovely house, eating delicious, home-cooked food. Every last crumb of it disappeared and Julian Harvey was heard to remark, rather plaintively, 'But I've only had a piece of garlic bread.' We noticed that the Hungarian actors who were also invited tucked into the food as appreciatively as we did, proving that actors are the same the world over.

ACTORS' FISH PIE

1 lb (450 g) smoked haddock, poached in milk, skinned and flaked
1 lb (450 g) fresh haddock, poached in milk, skinned and flaked
2 large hard-boiled eggs, sliced
2–4 oz (50–110 g) peeled prawns
12 baby mushrooms, sautéed in a little butter
FOR THE SAUCE
approx. 2 oz (50 g) butter or margarine
approx. 1½ oz (40 g) flour
¾ pint (425 ml) milk, reserved and strained after cooking the fish
freshly ground black pepper
FOR THE TOPPING
2–3 lb (450–900 g) potatoes, freshly mashed and well seasoned
extra butter or margarine
2–3 tomatoes, sliced

Lay the flaked fish in a buttered ovenproof dish. Place the sliced eggs on the fish then add the prawns and sautéed mushrooms. Make a white sauce by melting the butter in a saucepan over a low heat, adding the flour, and stirring with a wooden spoon for 1–2 minutes. Remove from the heat and add the warm cooking milk a few tablespoons at a time, stirring all the time (this makes it easier to achieve a lump-free sauce). When all the milk is added return the saucepan to a low heat and continue to stir until the sauce thickens. Season with pepper (you are unlikely to need salt when using smoked fish).

Cover the fish mixture with the white sauce. Top with a thick layer of mashed potato, arrange the sliced tomatoes over the top and dot with butter. Place in a preheated medium oven – 190°C (375°F) gas mark 5

– for 25–30 minutes until the fish is heated through and the potato topping is nicely browned. (If you prepare the dish in advance of cooking you will need to cook it longer to ensure that the fish is properly heated through.) Serve with a crisp salad or freshly cooked green vegetables.

To achieve perfection fish should swim three times – in water, in butter and in wine.

POLISH PROVERB

2 June 1660
All the afternoon with two or three captains in the Captain's cabin, drinking of white wine and sugar and eating pickled oysters – where Captain Sparling tells us the best Story that ever I heard; about a gentleman that persuaded a country fellow to let him gut his oysters or else they would stink.

SAMUEL PEPYS, *DIARY*

In Praise of Fish

Much do I love, at civic treat,
The monsters of the deep to eat;
To see the rosy salmon lying,
By smelts encircled, born for frying;
And from the china boat to pour,
On flaky cod, the flavour'd shower.
Thee, above all, I much regard,
Flatter than Longman's flattest bard,
Much honour'd turbot! – sore I grieve
Thee and thy dainty friends to leave.

SYDNEY SMITH, 1771–1845

The Ballad of Bouillabaisse

A street there is in Paris famous,
For which no rhyme our language yields,
Rue Neuve des Petits Champs its name is –
The New Street of the Little Fields;
And here's an inn, not rich and splendid,
But still in comfortable case;
The which in youth I often attended,
To eat a bowl of Bouillabaisse.

This Bouillabaisse a noble dish is –
A sort of soup or broth or brew,
Or hotchpotch, of all sorts of fishes,
That Greenwich never could outdo;
Green herbs, red peppers, mussels, saffern,
Soles, onions, garlic, roach and dace;
All these you eat at Terré's tavern,
In that one dish of Bouillabaisse.
Indeed, a rich and savoury stew 'tis;
And true philosophers methinks,
Who love all sorts of natural beauties,
Should love good victuals and good drinks.
And Cordelier or Benedictine
Mighty gladly, sure, his lot embrace,
Nor find a fast-day too afflicting
Which served him up a Bouillabaisse.

WILLIAM MAKEPEACE THACKERAY

———•———

This piece of cod passes all understanding.

SIR EDWIN LUTYENS, 1869–1944 (ATTRIBUTED)

———•———

The cream and hot butter mingled and overflowed, separating each glaucous bead of caviar from its fellows, capping it in white and gold.

EVELYN WAUGH, *BRIDESHEAD REVISITED*, 1945

———•———

THE KIPPER
For half a century, man and nipper,
I've doted on a tasty kipper,
But since I am no Jack the Ripper
I wish the kipper had a zipper.

OGDEN NASH

FOOD

The farmer has brown bread as fresh as day,
And butter fragrant as the dew of May,
Cornwall Squab-pie, and Devon white-pot brings,
And Lei'ster beans and bacon, food for kings!

TRADITIONAL

I don't care what I eat; what a confession to make! Is it not the same as
saying: 'I don't care whether I am dirty or clean'?

NORMAN DOUGLAS, *ALONE*, 1921

ON FOOD

Alas! What various tastes in food,
Divide the human brotherhood!
Birds in their little nests agree
With chinamen, but not with me.
Colonials like their oysters hot,
Their omelettes heavy – I do not.
The French are fond of slugs and frogs,
The Siamese eat puppy-dogs.

The Spaniard, I have heard it said,
Eats garlic by itself, on bread;
Now just suppose a friend or dun
Dropped in to lunch at half-past one
And you were jovially to say,
'Here's bread and garlic! Peg away!'
I doubt if you would gain your end
Or soothe the dun, or please the friend.

The nobles at the brilliant Court
Of Muscovy consumed a sort
Of candles held and eaten thus
As though they were asparagus.
In Italy the traveller notes
With great disgust the flesh of goats
Appearing on the table d'hôtes;
And even this the natives spoil
By frying it in rancid oil.

In Maryland they charge like sin
For nasty stuff called terrapin;
And when they ask you out to dine
At Washington, instead of wine,
They give you water from the spring
With lumps of ice for flavouring,
That sometimes kill and always freeze
The high plenipotentiaries.

In Massachusetts all the way
From Boston down to Buzzards Bay
They feed you till you want to die
On rhubarb pie and pumpkin pie,
And horrible huckleberry pie,
And when you summon strength to cry,

'What is there else that I can try?'
They stare at you in mild surprise
And serve you other kinds of pies.

And I with these mine eyes have seen
A dreadful stuff called Margarine
Consumed by men in Bethnal Green.

But I myself that here complain
Confess restriction quite in vain.
I feel my native courage fail
To see a Gascon eat a snail;
I dare not ask abroad for tea;
No cannibal can dine with me;
And all the world is torn and rent
By varying views on nutriment.
And yet upon the other hand,
De gustibus non disputand –
– Um.

HILAIRE BELLOC, 1870–1953

Some people have a foolish way of not minding, or pretending not to mind, what they eat. For my part, I mind my belly very studiously and very carefully; for I look upon it that he who does not mind his belly will hardly mind anything else.

DR JOHNSON IN JAMES BOSWELL, *LIFE OF SAMUEL JOHNSON,* 1791

Some hae meat and canna eat
And some wad eat that want it;
But we hae meat and we can eat,
And sae the Lord be thankit.

ROBERT BURNS, *THE SELKIRK GRACE*

The discovery of a new dish does more for human happiness than the discovery of a new star.

ANTHELME BRILLAT-SAVARIN, *PHYSIOLOGIE DU GOÛT*, 1825

A good pie is excellent when hot; but the *test* of a good pie is, 'How does it eat cold?'

WILLIAM MAGINN, *MAXIMS OF SIR WILLIAM O'DOHERTY, BART.*, 1849

It is good for a man to eat thistles, and to remember that he is an ass. But an artichoke is the best of thistles, and the man who enjoys it has the satisfaction of feeling that he is an ass of taste.

E. S. DALLAS, *KETTNER'S BOOK OF THE TABLE*, 1877

There is no love sincerer than the love of food.

GEORGE BERNARD SHAW, *MAN AND SUPERMAN*, 1903

EAT *v.i.* To perform successively (and successfully) the functions of mastication, humectation and deglutition.

AMBROSE BIERCE, *THE DEVIL'S DICTIONARY*, 1911

The egg is smooth and very pale;
It has no nose, it has no tail,
It has no ears that one can see;
It has no wit, no repartee.

ROY BISHOP, *THE INEFFICACIOUS EGG*

Grub first, then ethics.

BERTOLT BRECHT, 1898–1956

Food is an important part of a balanced diet.

FRAN LEBOWITZ

FRIENDSHIP

W e know that actors can sometimes seem over-theatrical and insin-
cere in their friendships, especially when they are in a large
group, and this has caused them to be labelled – rather unfairly in our
view – as 'luvvies'. It's true that theatrical conversations do tend to be
sprinkled with far too many 'darling's but the far from glamorous expla-
nation is that actors tend to meet and work with a lot of different people
and 'darling' is a pretty useful word when you can't remember the name
of the person you're talking to!

Intense friendships positively thrive in our line of business. A group
of people are thrown together to work on a project – a play, a television programme or a film – in circumstances that they find fairly
nerve-racking, even if they don't suffer from actual stage-fright. The
group clings together for mutual support, and strong bonds are formed.
It's a very, very pale reflection of the sort of thing that happens during

a war or a natural disaster and, perhaps because the actor's job is to portray emotions, we tend to express ourselves more theatrically and effusively than most. But real and enduring friendships *are* formed which last even when people don't see each other often. We have deep-rooted friendships with actors who worked with us in our repertory days, and when we *do* meet up it's almost as though we have been together all the time.

There's also an assumption that actors are terribly bitchy and will do each other down. This does happen of course, but time and again we have found that actors have great generosity and are kind and supportive of one another. Despite what people think, there may well be more bitchiness in your average office than in the theatre or studio. Certainly for us the camaraderie of working together in a group, all sharing the common aim of getting the show on the road, is one of the great pleasures of our profession.

A faithful friend is the medicine of life.

ECCLESIASTICUS

True friends visit us in prosperity only when invited, but in adversity they come without invitation.

THEOPHRASTUS C. 372–287 BC

A friendship will be young after a lapse of a century. A passion is old at the end of three months.

NIGU

Those friends thou hast, and their adoption tried,
Grapple them unto thy soul with hoops of steel.

WILLIAM SHAKESPEARE, *HAMLET* (ACT 1 SCENE 3) 1600–1601

A principal fruit of friendship is the ease and discharge of the fulness of the heart, which passions of all kinds do cause and induce. We know diseases of stoppings and suffocations are the most dangerous in the body; and it is not much otherwise in the mind; you may take sarza to open the liver, steel to open the spleen, flower of sulphur for the lungs, castoreum for the brain; but no recipe openeth the heart but a true friend to whom you may impart griefs, joys, fears, hopes, suspicions, counsels, and whatsoever lieth upon the heart to oppress it.

SIR FRANCIS BACON, *ESSAYS*, 1625

The mind never unbends itself so agreeably as in the conversation of a well-chosen friend. There is indeed no blessing of life that is in any way comparable to the enjoyment of a discreet and virtuous friend. It eases and unloads the mind, clears and improves the understanding, engenders thoughts and knowledge, animates virtue and good resolutions, soothes and allays the passions, and finds employment for most of the vacant hours of life.

JOSEPH ADDISON, 1672–1719

To friendship every burden's light.

JOHN GAY, 1685–1732

Be slow in choosing a friend, slower in changing.

BENJAMIN FRANKLIN, 1706–90

I mentioned my expectations from the interest of an eminent person then in power; adding; 'but I have no claim but the claim of friendship; however, some people will go a great way for that motive.'
Johnson. 'Sir, they will go all the way for that motive.'

JAMES BOSWELL, *LIFE OF SAMUEL JOHNSON*, 1791

If a man does not make new friendships as he advances through life, he will soon find himself left alone. A man should keep his friendships in constant repair.

DR JOHNSON IN JAMES BOSWELL, *LIFE OF SAMUEL JOHNSON*, 1791

Love is flower-like;
Friendship is like a sheltering tree.

SAMUEL TAYLOR COLERIDGE, 1772–1834

128

A fashionable friend is one who will dine with you, game with you, walk or ride out with you, borrow money of you, escort your wife to public places – if she be handsome, stand by and see you fairly shot if you happen to be engaged in a duel, and slink away and see you fairly clapped in prison, if you experience a reverse of fortunes. Such a man is like the shadow of the sundial, which appears in fine weather, and vanishes when there comes a rainy day.

HORACE SMITH, 1775–1839

It may be worth noticing, as a curious circumstance, when persons past forty before they were at all acquainted, form together a very close intimacy of friendship. For grafts of old wood to take, there must be a wonderful congeniality between the trees.

RICHARD WHATELY, 1787–1863

Friendship that flows from the heart cannot be frozen in adversity, as the water that flows from the spring cannot congeal in winter.

JAMES FENIMORE COOPER, 1789–1851

True friendship is like sound health, the value of it is seldom known until it be lost.

CHARLES CALEB COLTON, *LACON, OR MANY THINGS IN FEW WORDS,* 1822

We can live without a brother, but not without a friend.

GERMAN PROVERB

I would not live without the love of my friends.

JOHN KEATS, 1795–1821

There is no folly equal to that of throwing away friendship in a world where friendship is rare.

EDWARD BULWER-LYTTON, 1803–73

Friendship is the bread of the heart.

MARY RUSSELL MITFORD, 1787–1855

The only way to have a friend, is to be one.

RALPH WALDO EMERSON, 1803–82

A female friend, amiable, clever, and devoted, is a possession more valuable than parks and palaces; and without such a muse few men can succeed in life, none be contented.

BENJAMIN DISRAELI, 1804–91

A difference of taste in jokes is a great strain on the affections.

GEORGE ELIOT, 1819–80

Alter? When the hills do.
Falter? When the sun
Question if his glory
Be the perfect one.

Surfeit? When the daffodil
Doth of the dew:
Even as herself, O friend!
I will of you!

EMILY DICKINSON, 1830–86

'Stay,' is a charming word in a friend's vocabulary.

LOUISA MAY ALCOTT, 1832–88

Friendship gives no privilege to make ourselves disagreeable.

SIR JOHN LUBBOCK, 1834–1913

I always felt that the great high privilege, relief and comfort of friendship, was that one had to explain nothing.

KATHERINE MANSFIELD, 1888–1923

Sudden friendships generally come to sudden ends. True friendship is a plant of gradual growth, which needs for its perfection sun and air, watering and weeding.

KATHERINE E. CONWAY

A reverse of fortune is a mighty sifter of friendship.

H. R. HARWEIS

If you would keep your friend, approach him with a telescope, never with a microscope.

ANON

When Socrates was building himself a house at Athens, being asked by one that observed the littleness of the design why a man so eminent would not have an abode more suitable to his dignity, he replied that he should think himself sufficiently accommodated if he could see that narrow habitation filled with real friends.

DR JOHNSON IN JAMES BOSWELL, *LIFE OF SAMUEL JOHNSON*, 1791

HAPPINESS

Be wise, decant the wine, prune back
your long-term hopes. Life ebbs as I speak:
so seize each day, and grant the next no credit.

HORACE, 65–8 BC

FROM ODE TO A NIGHTINGALE
O, for a draught of vintage! that hath been
Cooled a long age in the deep-delvèd earth,
Tasting of Flora and the country-green,
Dance, and Provençal song, and sunburnt mirth!
O for a beaker full of the warm South,
Full of the true, the blushful Hippocrene,
With beaded bubbles winking at the brim,
And purple-stainèd mouth,
That I might drink, and leave the world unseen,
And with thee fade away into the forest dim –

JOHN KEATS, 1795–1821

MR HARDCASTLE. I love everything that's old: old friends, old times, old manners, old books, old wine; and I believe, Dorothy *(taking her hand)*, you'll own I have been pretty fond of an old wife.

OLIVER GOLDSMITH, SHE STOOPS TO CONQUER, 1773

The happiest part of a man's life is what he passes lying awake in bed in the morning.

DR JOHNSON IN JAMES BOSWELL, LIFE OF SAMUEL JOHNSON, 1791

My idea of heaven is eating *foie gras* to the sound of trumpets.

SYDNEY SMITH, 1771–1845

A comfortable house is a great source of happiness. It ranks immediately after health and a good conscience.

SYDNEY SMITH, 1771–1845

All he [Skimpole] asked of society was, to let him live. *That* wasn't much. His wants were few. Give him the papers, conversation, music, mutton, coffee, landscape, fruit in the season, a few sheet of Bristol-board, and a little claret and he asked no more. He was a mere child in the world. 'Go your several ways in peace! Wear red coats, blue coats, lawn sleeves, put pens behind your ears, wear aprons; go after glory, holiness, commerce, trade, any object you prefer; only – let Harold Skimpole live!'

CHARLES DICKENS, *BLEAK HOUSE*, 1853

Remember, I do not recommend motion at all. Repose is my idea of life; repose and grapes.

ANTHONY TROLLOPE, *PHINEAS FINN*, 1869

A good cigar is as great a comfort to a man as a good cry is to a woman.

EDWARD BULWER-LYTTON, 1803–73

If only we'd stop trying to be happy, we could have a pretty good time.

EDITH WHARTON C. 1861–1937

O I HAVE DINED ON THIS DELICIOUS DAY

O I have dined on this delicious day,
on green-salad treetops wet with beaded
water, tossed by the fork tines of the wind;
devoured the crouton water-birds and
every crumb and crust of the dark-bread earth;
through gristle to the marrowbone of rocks
and the wrinkled grain of high-loaf hills – all
garnished by kindled bush and window grass.

O I have bitten into this bright day
and drunk from the clean basin of its sky
till only the clouds were left clinging to
my glass and the sun turned on its spit
into grape-press night and finished with
a frosted melon-ball of yellow moon.

RICHARD SNYDER

HOSPITALITY

Let my quarrymen receive these cakes, wine, bread, barley, fish and beans. Let their hearts be happy and their arms be strong.

Pharaoh Rameses II, Command carved at the granite quarries of Wadi Hamammat, c.1270 BC

A host is like a general: it takes a mishap to reveal his genius.

Horace, 65–8 BC

Rebuke to a Guest Who Failed to Appear

How happened it, my friend, that you did not keep your engagement the other night to sup with me? But take notice, justice is to be had, and I expect you shall fully reimburse me the expense I was at to treat you; which, let me tell, was no small sum. I had prepared, you must know, a lettuce apiece, three snails, two eggs, and a barley cake, with some sweet wine and snow, the snow most certainly I shall charge to your account, as a rarity that will not keep. Besides all these curious dishes, there were olives of Andalusia, gourds, shallots, and a hundred other dainties equally sumptuous. You should likewise have been entertained either with an interlude, the rehearsal of a poem or a piece of music, as you liked best; or (such was my liberality) with all three. But the luxurious delicacies and Spanish dancers, of a certain – I know not who – were, it seems, more to your taste. However, I shall have my revenge on you, depend upon it; in what manner shall be at present a secret. In good truth it was not kind thus to mortify your friend – I had almost said yourself, and, upon second thoughts, I do say so: for how agreeably should we have spent the evening, in laughing, trifling, and deep speculation! You may sup, I confess, at many places more splendidly, but you can nowhere be treated with more unconstrained cheerfulness, simplicity, and freedom; only make the experiment; and if you do not ever afterwards prefer my table to any other, never favour me with your company again. Farewell.

PLINY THE YOUNGER (62–113) TO SEPTIMUS CLARUS

It will never do, Sir. There is nothing served about there, neither tea, nor coffee, nor lemonade, nor anything whatever; and depend upon it, Sir, a man does not love to go to a place from whence he comes out exactly as he went in.

DR SAMUEL JOHNSON, 1709–84

HOSPITALITY IS A MOST EXCELLENT VIRTUE; but care must be taken that the love of company, for its own sake, does not become a prevailing passion; for then the habit is no longer hospitality, but dissipation. Reality and truthfulness in this, as in all other duties of life, are the points to be studied; for as Washington Irving well says – 'There is an emanation from the heart in genuine hospitality which cannot be described, but is immediately felt, and puts the stranger at once at his ease.' With respect to the continuance of acquaintanceships, however, it may be found necessary, in some cases, for a mistress to relinquish, on assuming the responsibility of a household, many of those commenced in the earlier parts of her life. This will be the more requisite if the number still retained be quite equal to her means and opportunities.

MRS BEETON, MRS BEETON'S BOOK OF HOUSEHOLD MANAGEMENT, 1861

Gastronomical perfection can be reached in these combinations: one person dining alone, usually upon a couch or a hillside; two persons, of no matter what age or sex, dining in a good restaurant; six people, of no matter what sex or age, dining in a good home. The six should be capable of decent social behaviour; that is, no two of them should be so much in love as to bore the others, nor, at the opposite extreme, should they be carrying on any sexual or professional feud which could put poison in the plates all must eat from. A good combination would be one married couple, for warm composure; one less firmly established, to add a note of investigation to the talk; and two strangers of either sex, upon whom the better acquainted could sharpen their questioning wits. Hunger and fair to good basic health are basic requirements, for no man stayed by a heavy mid-afternoon snack or gnawed by a gastric ulcer can add much to the general well-being.

M. F. K. FISHER

———

I remember the dinner well – soup of *oseille,* a sole quite simply cooked in a white-wine sauce, a *caneton à la presse,* a lemon soufflé. At the last minute, fearing that the whole thing was too simple for Rex, I added *caviar aux blinis.* And for wine I let him give me a bottle of 1906 Montrachet, then at its prime, and, with the duck, a Clos de Bèze of 1904.

EVELYN WAUGH, *BRIDESHEAD REVISITED,* 1945

Friendliness and easy hospitality are more important than grandeur.

CONSTANCE SPRY, *THE CONSTANCE SPRY COOKERY BOOK*, 1956

GATECRASHER

There was this well-behaved party,
'Oh, thank you' said everybody
to the hostess and the host,
accepting pâté
on slim slivers of toast
with sliced olives,
and crystal goblets of wine,
it was a mine-
field for the clumsy.
Then all of a sudden
the door burst open
and a man fell into the velvety room.
'Wotcha, folks' he bellowed, plonking his hat
onto a perfectly coiffured head, whereat
he swigged alcohol,
stuffed himself with food,
sang at the top of his voice,
grabbed a horrified woman,
kissed her and pinched her bum,
then all of a sudden he left
as suddenly as he'd come.
Said one appalled girl to her friend,
'Who was that *awful* man?
He's made Eleanor cry.'
'Oh, don't be silly,' replied her friend,
'he's all right really,
he's just shy.'

CHARLOTTE MITCHELL © 1991

HOSTELRIES AND RESTAURANTS

Michael Gambon and I became great friends while working on a sitcom called *The Other One,* written by the splendid John Esmonde and Bob Larbey. We thought it would be fun to do a stage play together and that *Uncle Vanya* would be a challenging piece to take on. A well-known impresario showed interest and invited us to lunch to discuss the project at a very posh restaurant in Covent Garden, which specialized in fashionable nouvelle cuisine. As the meal progressed Mike, who is a first-class trencherman, whispered, 'Why are all the dishes starters, Dick?' 'Nouvelle cuisine, old man,' I replied knowledgeably. 'Delicious food but small portions.'

When the lunch was over we thanked our host and walked together towards the Tube. 'Well, that was a delightful lunch,' I said. 'Terrific, Dick,' said Mike, 'but if you'll just excuse me I'm going to nip round the corner for a plate of sausage and chips.'

I'm sure he would have been much happier in the sort of old-fashioned inn where a warm welcome, good cheer and hearty fare were always on offer. Fashions may come and go but a welcoming inn is always popular, as this piece written some three hundred years ago reminds us.

The weather being wet, and my two-legged horse being almost tired (for indeed my own legs were all the supporters that my body had), I went dripping into an alehouse; there found I, first a kind welcome, next good liquor, then kind strangers (which made good company), then an honest host, whose love to good liquor was written in red characters both in his nose, cheeks and forehead: an hostess I found there too, a woman of very good carriage; and though she had not so much colour (for what she had done) as her rich husband, yet all beholders might perceive by the roundness of her belly, that she was able to draw a pot dry at a draught, and ne'er unlace for the matter.

ANON, SEVENTEENTH CENTURY

6 March 1660 Shove-tuesday
Here comes my uncle Thom., who I took to Wills and drank with... While we were drinking, in comes Mr Day, a Carpenter in Westminister, to tell me that it was Shrove-tuesday and that I must go with him to their yearly club upon this day, which I confess I had quite forgot. So I went to the Bell, where was Mr's Eglin, Veezy, Vincent a butcher, one more, and Mr Tanner, with whom I played upon a viall and he the viallin after dinner, and we were very merry, with a special good dinner – a leg of veal and bacon, two capons and sausages and fritters, with abundance of wine.

SAMUEL PEPYS, *Diary*

Few among those who go to restaurants realize that the man who first opened one must have been a man of genius and a profound observer.

ANTHELME BRILLAT-SAVARIN, *PHYSIOLOGIE DU GOÛT*, 1825

———

It was a large room with some large maps in it. I doubt if I could have felt much stranger if the maps had been real foreign countries, and I cast away in the middle of them. I felt it was taking a liberty to sit down, with my cap in my hand, on the corner of the chair nearest the door; and when the waiter laid a cloth on purpose for me, and put a set of casters on it, I think I must have turned red all over with modesty.

He brought me some chops and vegetables, and took the covers off in such a bouncing manner that I was afraid I must have given him some offence. But he greatly relieved my mind by putting a chair for me at the table, and saying, very affably, 'Now, six-foot! come on!'

I thanked him and took my seat at the board; but found it extremely difficult to handle my knife and fork with anything like dexterity, or to avoid splashing myself with gravy while he was standing opposite, staring so hard, and making me blush in the most dreadful manner every time I caught his eye. After watching me into the second chop, he said:

'There's half a pint of ale for you. Will you have it now?'

I thanked him and said 'yes'. Upon which he poured it out of a jug into a large tumbler, and held it up against the light and made it look beautiful.

'My eye!' he said. 'It seems a good deal, don't it?'

'It does seem a good deal,' I answered with a smile. For it was quite delightful to me to find him so pleasant. He was a twinkling-eyed, pimple-faced man, with his hair standing upright all over his head; and as he stood with one arm a-kimbo, holding up the glass to the light with the other hand, he looked quite friendly.

'There was a gentleman here, yesterday,' he said – 'a stout gentleman by the name of Topsawyer – perhaps you know him?'

'No,' I said, 'I don't think –'

'In breeches and gaiters, broad-brimmed hat, grey coat, speckled choker,' said the waiter. 'No,' I said bashfully, 'I haven't the pleasure –'

'He came in here,' said the waiter, looking at the light through the tumbler, 'ordered a glass of this ale – *would* order it – I told him not – drank it, and fell down dead. It was too old for him. It oughtn't to be drawn; that's the fact.'

I was very much shocked to hear of this melancholy accident, and said I thought I had better have some water.

'Why you see,' said the waiter, still looking at the light through the tumbler, with one of his eyes shut up, 'our people don't like things being ordered and left. It offends 'em. But *I'll* drink it, if you like. I'm used to it, and use is everything. I don't think it'll hurt me, if I throw my head back, and take it off quick. Shall I?'

I replied that he would much oblige me by drinking it, if he thought he could do it safely, but by no means otherwise. When he did throw his head back, and take it off quick, I had a horrible fear, I confess, of seeing him meet the fate of the lamented Mr Topsawyer, and fall life-less on the carpet. But it didn't hurt him. On the contrary, I thought he seemed the fresher for it.

'What have we got here?' he said, putting a fork into my dish. 'Not chops?'

'Chops,' I said.

'Lord bless my soul!' he exclaimed. 'I didn't know they were chops. Why a chop's the very thing to take off the bad effects of that beer! Ain't it lucky?'

So he took a chop by the bone in one hand, and a potato in the other, and ate away with a very good appetite, to my extreme satisfaction. He afterwards took another chop, and another potato. When he had done, he brought me a pudding, and having set it before me, seemed to rumi-nate, and to become absent in his mind for some moments.

'How's the pie?' he said, rousing himself.

'It's a pudding,' I made answer.

'Pudding!' he exclaimed. 'Why, bless me, so it is! What!' Looking at it nearer. 'You don't mean to say it's a batter pudding!'

'Yes, it is indeed.'

'Why, a batter pudding,' he said, taking up a table-spoon, 'is my favourite pudding! Ain't that lucky? Come on, little 'un, and let's see who'll get most.'

The waiter certainly got most. He entreated me more than once to come in and win, but what with the table-spoon to my teaspoon, his despatch to my despatch, and his appetite to my appetite, I was left far behind at the first mouthful, and had no chance with him. I never saw anyone enjoy a pudding so much, I think. And he laughed, when it was all gone, as if his enjoyment of it lasted still.

CHARLES DICKENS, *DAVID COPPERFIELD*, 1850

At the Brunnenthal Peacock it is necessary that you should believe in the paramount importance of dinner. Not to come to it at the appointed time would create, first marvel, in the Frau's mind, then pity, – as to the state of your health, – and at last hot anger should it be found that such neglect arose from contempt. What muse will assist me to describe these dinners in a few words? They were commenced of course by soup, – real soup, not barley broth with a strong prevalence of the barley. Then would follow the boiled meats, from which the soup was supposed to have been made, – but such boiled meat, so good, that the supposition must have contained a falsehood. With this there would be always potatoes and pickled cabbages and various relishes. Then there would be two other kinds of meat, generally with accompaniment of stewed fruit; after that fish, – trout from the neighbouring stream, for the preservation of which great tanks had been made. Vegetables with unknown sauces would follow, – and then would come the roast, which consisted always of poultry, and was accompanied of course by salad. But it was after this that were made the efforts on which the Frau's fame most depended. The puddings, I think, were the subject of her greatest struggles and most complete success. Two puddings daily were, by the rules of the house, required to be eaten; not two puddings brought together so that you might choose with careless haste either one or the other; but two separate courses of puddings, with an interval between for

appreciation, for thought, and for digestion. Either one or both can, no doubt, be declined. No absolute punishment – such as notice to leave the house, – follows such abstention. But the Frau is displeased, and when dressed in her best on Sundays does not smile on those who abstain. After the puddings there is dessert, and there are little cakes to nibble if you will. They are nibbled very freely. But the heat of the battle is over with the second pudding.

ANTHONY TROLLOPE, *WHY FRAU FROHMANN RAISED HER PRICES*, 1877

Any two meals at a boarding-house are together less than two square meals.

STEPHEN LEACOCK, *LITERARY LAPSES*, 1910

The counter, sheathed in a case of pewter, the glasses all in a row, the sleek barrels and irregular lines of home-brewed cordials, charmed the casual visitor to a more intimate acquaintance. Behind the tap was the Travellers' Room, and what a room it was – with great open fireplaces and spits and bubbling kettles and blackened ingles. Long-buried ancestors of the village had carved their rude initials over each high-backed bench and battered the bottoms of the great tankards into unexpected dents by many rollicking choruses in the merry dead past. The walls of this room knew the pedigree of every bullock and the legend of every ghost for miles around. Here was the cleanest floor, the clearest fire in England.

Old Tabrum the landlord was the very man for the house – the very man to bring out all the most worthy in his guests. He always produced good wine and a piping hot supper, never asked for his money till his guests were satisfied, and wore an apron as white as the foam of his cool deep ale.

He was eighty years old now, with a bloom on his cheeks like an Autumn pippin and two limpid blue eyes that looked straight into yours and, if you had any reverence at all, made the tears well involuntarily at the sight of such gentle beauty.

COMPTON MACKENZIE, *THE PASSIONATE ELOPEMENT*, 1911

I had arrived in Rhyl and was lodging in West Parade on the sea front. The meals were not grand, and having had another rise in salary (to, I think, six pounds a week) I was feeling flush and thought I would treat myself to a slap-up meal. I bought myself eight ounces of best fillet steak and some beautiful asparagus, presenting them to my landlady, a genuine but simple soul, with instructions that after seeing the present show at the Pavilion, I would be home to dine at ten o'clock...

I hurried back to the digs, with the sea air in my nostrils, looking forward to my steak and asparagus.

'Oh, there you are, dear,' said the landlady. 'I bet you're hungry. I've made your meat into a lovely stew for you, and I've put your flowers in water.'

I sat alone, eating a fillet-steak stew, and staring at a bunch of asparagus in a glass vase. From then on, I ate what was put in front of me. Either that, or I went to the café along the front which advertised, *Egg and chips, one and sixpence, small children ninepence.* I never ordered the small children, but the egg and chips were excellent.

RONNIE BARKER, *DANCING IN THE MOONLIGHT*, 1993

——•——

A fire has destroyed the Chameleon at Strood,
Which makes me exceedingly glad;
For the waitresses there were disgustingly rude
And the food was incredibly bad.

MICHAEL POPE, *CAPITAL LEVITIES*

LUNCHEON

Luncheon, as a word of comprehensive meaning, may fairly take a high place, signifying as it does such a grand variety of meals, ranging from the simple 'glass of wine and a biscuit' or the more humble 'crust of bread and cheese and glass of ale' to an elaborate meal, that is in all but name, a dinner. Only one general meaning that the word has is that it stands for whatever is partaken between the last named meal and breakfast. Many are the arguments for and against luncheon, some right, some wrong no doubt: but for all that we have luncheon fully installed amongst our list of meals, and there it is likely to remain until the end of the chapter.

When the dinner hour is an early one, those who value their health will do well to avoid lunching; but when breakfast takes place at 8 or 9 and dinner is late, a substantial lunch may safely be indulged in, and is a most useful if not absolutely necessary meal.

These meals are naturally regulated by various circumstances such as individual taste, means and station; in a high class house, however, it is usual to serve a good repast, not alone for the family, but for the reason that, at an informal meal, chance guests have to be provided for.

HIGH CLASS LUNCHEONS. – At these anything and everything that is served for dinner, such as soup, fish, entrées, poultry, game or joints may be given, but a number of courses such as compose the latter meal are not in the least necessary, or even usual. Soup, in winter, is a welcome course, to be followed by any hot entrées, game or poultry, the joints, if any, being generally cold, two or three sweets, one of which may be some simple milk pudding, with cheese, biscuits, cake and fruit. In summer, the dishes may be either hot or cold or both, when salads should be added to the menu, and potatoes may be the only vegetable, these being chipped, mashed, or cooked in any way except plainly boiled. Fish is more common at dinner than luncheon, unless it be in the form

of croquettes or rissoles, filleted soles, and mayonnaise of salmon or lobster.

MIDDLE CLASS LUNCHEONS. – Where there is a nursery these generally serve for the children's dinner, and in consequence the chief dishes are simple and substantial, often consisting of a joint and a pudding. When the children do not share the meal, a joint which is cooked for the kitchen dinner is often brought first into the dining room, but this is not a custom to be commended, for the reason that the servants have their chief meal late and cold. So many nice little dishes can be made from cold meats left from the preceding day, that those who like hot luncheons need not trespass on the servants' dinner.

MRS BEETON, *MRS BEETON'S BOOK OF HOUSEHOLD MANAGEMENT*, 1861

Angela Brazil's account of three plucky schoolgirls trying to cook lunch for their teachers is a mixture of triumph and despair. It brought back our own blithely confident early attempts to impress parents and friends by our culinary skills, only to find out that creating a perfect meal is by no means as easy as it looks when accomplished by more experienced hands. The scene is set in the little cottage where the girls of the Grange take it in turns to organize a day of 'domestic economy'. Now read on…

The list of dishes looked quite imposing and elegant when written in a foreign language. Aldred regarded it with pride, and copied it in her best handwriting:

MENU
Potage aux Herbes
Côtelettes de Mouton aux Légumes
Sauce Anglaise
Pommes de Terre au Naturel
Haricots Verts
Blancmange
Pâte de Prunes
Fromage
Dessert
Café

… 'A six-course dinner!' exclaimed Miss Drummond picking up the menu with great approval. 'This is more than Mademoiselle and I had dreamed of! We certainly never expected to find soup – it is quite a surprise! Where did you get the stock?'

'There wasn't any stock; it's made from vegetables,' replied Aldred. 'I heard a French lady tell my aunt how to do it, so I thought I'd try.'

'*Potage aux herbes!*' ejaculated Mademoiselle, looking at the tureen with an interest half-gastronomical, half-sentimental; 'ah, but that bring to me other days! I have not tasted *bouillon maigre* since I live with my grand'mère at Avignon.'

'You must imagine you are back in Provence, then, Mademoiselle,' said Miss Drummond, as she helped to hand the plates.

'It was a sweet thought to make it – *une idée tout à fait gentille!* The scenes of one's youth, ah, what it is to recall them to memory! *Ma foi!* but I am again in the old white *château:* the green shutters are closed to keep out the warm sun; *Jules, the concierge,* carries in the dishes, treading softly on the polished floor; outside is the cooing of doves, and the tinkling of goat bells. *Grand'mère,* so stately, so erect, so gay in spite of her years, she sit at the table's head, and serve to all the portion. It is to me as if I were there!'

Steeped in these reminiscences of her childhood Mademoiselle, with pleased anticipation, raised her spoon to her lips. Then, alas! alas! she spluttered, made a horrible grimace, and buried her face in her serviette.

'Ah! *mais c'est dégoûtant!*' she murmured faintly.

Aldred hurried to taste her own plateful. Mademoiselle had not exaggerated matters: a more unpleasant brew could not be imagined. The various vegetables and herbs were still half-raw, and had not imparted their flavour, so the soup seemed mainly a mixture of spices and salad oil, and had, besides, a suggestion of paraffin, owing no doubt to the flaring-up of the stove.

Poor Aldred blushed hotly. She was covered with confusion at such a dead failure. The others had all politely sampled the soup, and then laid down their spoons; it was quite impossible for anybody to take it.

'Never mind, my dear!' said Miss Drummond kindly. 'You have tried to give us a surprise, and we are as sorry as you that it should have turned out so unfortunately. Even the best cook has to profit by experience, and the value of this little cottage is that it gives you the opportunity of learning from practice. You will be wiser another time. Perhaps your aunt's friend will send you a written recipe, with exact quantities and instructions. It needs a very old housekeeper to make a dish from hearsay. Suppose you take out the tureen, and we will go on with the next course.'

Mabel's and Dora's stew, made exactly as Miss Reade had shown them in the cookery class, was quite satisfactory. They had put in the right seasoning, and had remembered to brown and thicken the gravy. The potatoes and beans were also up to standard, which cheered Aldred a little. She was partly responsible for them, and had helped to prepare them, though it was Dora who had shaken the potato pan, and put a dab of butter among the beans. Miss Drummond looked mildly surprised at the addition of bread sauce, but she helped herself without comment, feeling pledged to taste all her pupils' efforts. Aldred had been obliged to draw upon her inventive powers for this also, as she had no recipe, and the result, though not so disagreeable as the soup, was far from palatable. She had made it exactly like bread and milk, without onion, butter, or cloves; and had even added a little sugar to it. She wished sincerely she had not included it in the menu, or, at any rate, that she had not allowed it to be brought to table. She looked so conscious and distressed that Miss Drummond readily divined who was the author of the attempt, and charitably forbore to remark upon it, though she left her portion unfinished on her plate.

The rest of the dinner was really very creditable. Dora's blancmange was smooth, and Mabel's pastry light. Aldred had arranged the cheese and biscuits daintily on paper doyleys; and the coffee, a combined effort of the trio, was a great improvement upon that of the morning.

The three girls heaved a vast sigh of relief when Miss Drummond, after a tour of inspection into the kitchen and scullery, departed, expressing satisfaction both with the dinner and with the general neatness and order of the establishment. Mademoiselle had excused herself the moment the coffee was finished.

ANGELA BRAZIL, *A FOURTH FORM FRIENDSHIP*, 1911

The schoolgirls' well-meaning attempt at an elegant lunch party, requiring such a generous scattering of exclamation marks in the telling, makes an interesting contrast with the effortless smoothness and comfort of lunch at High Table at a Cambridge college as described by Virginia Woolf.

The lunch on this occasion began with soles, sunk in a deep dish, over which the college cook had spread a counterpane of the whitest cream, save that it was branded here and there with brown spots like the spots on the flanks of a doe. After that came the partridges, but if this suggests a couple of bald, brown birds on a plate you are mistaken. The partridges, many and various, came with all their retinue of sauces and salads, the sharp and the sweet, each in its order; their potatoes, thin as coins but not so hard; their sprouts, foliated as rose-buds but more succulent. And no sooner had the roast and its retinue been done with than the silent serving man, the Beadle himself perhaps in a milder manifestation, set before us, wreathed in napkins, a confection which rose all sugar from the waves. To call it a pudding and so relate it to rice and tapioca would be an insult. Meanwhile the wine glasses had flushed yellow and flushed crimson; had been emptied; had been filled. And thus, by degrees was lit halfway down the spine, which is the seat of the soul, not that hard little electric light which we call brilliance, as it pops in and out upon our lips, but the more profound, subtle and subterranean glow which is the rich yellow flame of rational intercourse. No need to hurry. No need to sparkle. No need to be anybody but oneself. We are all going to heaven and Vandyck is of the company – in other words how good life seemed, how sweet its rewards, how trivial this grudge or that grievance, how admirable friendship and the society of one's kind, as, lighting a good cigarette, one sunk among the cushions in the window seat.

VIRGINIA WOOLF, *A ROOM OF ONE'S OWN,* 1929

MANGOES

—▸—

I love fruit in all its guises, whether it's raw or cooked. Richard, like so many men, is deeply suspicious of anything he thinks might be good for him and has to be coaxed into eating fruit; he tries to avoid it on the pretext that it is too acid. I suspect that the wine he loves may also have some connection with acidity, but let that be. We both agree that mangoes are absolutely delicious, and because of their marvellous flavour we are quite happy to put up with the appallingly sticky mess we get into while eating them.

This wonderfully suggestive poem about the way in which eating a mango breaks down your inhibitions was introduced to me at an Open University seminar, and has been a great favourite ever since.

—▸—

English Girl Eats Her First Mango
(a kind of love poem)

> If I did tell she
> hold this gold
> of sundizzy
> tonguelicking juicy
> mouthwater flow
> ripe with love
> from the tropics
>
> she woulda tell me
> trust you to be melodramatic
>
> so I just say
> taste this mango

and I watch she hold
the smooth cheeks
of the mango
blushing yellow
and a glow
rush to she own cheeks

and she ask me
what do I do now
just bite into it?

and I was tempted
to tell she why not be a devil
and eat of the skin
of original sin

but she woulda tell me
trust you to be
mysterious

so I just say
it's up to you
if you want to peel it

and I watch she feel it
as something precious
then she smile and say
looks delicious

and I tell she
don't waste sweet words
when sweetness
in your hand

just bite it man
peel it with the teeth
that God gave you

or better yet
do like me mother
used to do
and squeeze
till the flesh
turn syrup
nibble a hole
then suck the gold
like bubby
in child mouth
squeeze and tease out
every drop of spice

sounds nice
me friend tell me

and I remind she
that this ain't
apple core
so don't forget
the seed
suck that too
the sweetest part
the juice does run
down to your heart

man if you see
the English rose
she face was bliss
down to the pink

of she toes

and when she finish
she smile
and turn to me

lend me your hanky
my fingers
are all sticky
with mango juice

and I had to tell she
what hanky
you talking bout
you don't know
when you eat mango
you hanky
is you tongue

man just lick
you finger
you call that
culture
lick you finger
you call that
culture

unless you prefer
to call it
colonization
in reverse

JOHN AGARD, *MANGOES AND BULLETS*, 1985

MEAT

RECEIPT TO ROAST MUTTON
Gently Stir and blow the fire,
Lay the mutton down to roast,
Dress it quickly, I desire;
In the dripping put a toast,
That I hunger may remove; –
Mutton is the meat I love.

On the dresser see it lie;
Oh! the charming white and red!
Finer meat ne'er met the eye,
On the sweetest grass it fed;
Let the jack go swiftly round,
Let me have it nicely brown'd.

On the table spread the cloth,
Let the knives be sharp and clean,
Pickles get and salad both,
Let them each be fresh and green.
With small beer, good ale, and wine,
O ye gods! How shall I dine!

SYDNEY SMITH, 1771–1845

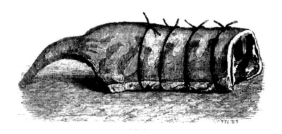

A couple of flitches of bacon are worth fifty thousand Methodist sermons and religious tracts. They are great softeners of temper and promoters of domestic harmony.

WILLIAM COBBETT, *COTTAGE ECONOMY*, 1821

Never you mind about the piece of needlework, the tambouring and the maps of the world made by her needle. Get to see her at work upon a mutton chop, or a bit of bread and cheese, and if she deal quickly with them, you have a pretty security for that activity, without which a wife is a burden instead of being a help.

WILLIAM COBBETT, *ADVICE TO YOUNG MEN*, 1830

Tongue; well, that's a wery good thing when it an't a woman's.

CHARLES DICKENS, *PICKWICK PAPERS*, 1837–9

'Kate, my dear,' said Mrs Nickleby; 'I don't know how it is, but a fine warm summer day like this, with the birds singing in every direction, always puts me in mind of roast pig, with sage and onion sauce and made gravy.'

'That's a curious association of ideas is it not, mamma?'

'Upon my word, my dear, I don't know,' replied Mrs Nickleby. 'Roast pig – let me see. On the day five weeks after you were christened, we had a roast – no that couldn't have been a pig, either, because I recollect there was a pair of them to carve, and your poor papa and I could never have thought of sitting down to two pigs – they must have been partridges. Roast pig! I hardly think we ever could have had one, now I come to remember, for your papa could never bear the sight of them in the shops, and used to say that they always put him in mind of very little babies, only the pigs had much fairer complexions; and he had a horror of little babies, too, because he couldn't very well afford any increase to his family, and had a natural dislike to the subject. It's very odd now, what can put that in my head! I recollect dining once at Mrs Bevan's, in that broad street, round the corner by the coachmaker's, where the tipsy man fell through the cellar-flap of an empty house nearly a week before the quarter-day, and wasn't found till the new tenant went in – and we had roast pig there. It must be that, I think, that reminds me of it, especially as there was a little bird in the room that would keep on singing all the time of dinner – at least, not a little bird, for it was a parrot, and he didn't sing exactly, for he talked and swore dreadfully; but I think it must be that. Indeed I am sure it must. Shouldn't you say so, my dear?'

CHARLES DICKENS, *NICHOLAS NICKLEBY*, 1839

Look at Pork. There's a subject! If you want a subject, look at Pork!

CHARLES DICKENS, *GREAT EXPECTATIONS*, 1860–61

Braemar, Scotland, 28 September, 1853.
I think it my duty to record the unmatched merits of a leg of mutton we had today at dinner. It was a leg which stands out even amidst all the legs of my long and steadily muttonised life. It was glorious. A leg of which the fat flats of England can have no idea, and which even Wales, in its most favoured circumstances, could only approach. It was a leg which told how it had strayed among mountains from its lambhood to its death. It spoke of winter straths and summer heights, of tender heather, Alpine airs, cold springs, and that short sweet grass which corries alone can cherish. These were the mettle of its pasture. It left its savour on the palate, like the savour of a good deed on the heart.

LORD COCKBURN, 1779–1854, *JOURNAL*

As for the leg of mutton it is truly wonderful; nothing so good had I ever tasted in the shape of a leg of mutton. The leg of mutton of Wales beats the leg of mutton of any other country, and I had never tasted a Welsh leg of mutton before. Certainly I shall never forget the first Welsh leg of mutton which I tasted, rich but delicate, replete with juices derived from the aromatic herbs of the noble Berwyn, cooked to a turn, and weighing just four pounds.

GEORGE BORROW, *WILD WALES*, 1862

… an exquisite scent of olives and oil and juice rose from the great brown dish as Marthe, with a little flourish, took the cover off. The cook had spent three days over that dish. And she must take great care, Mrs Ramsay thought, diving into the soft mass, to choose a specially tender piece for William Bankes. And she peered into the dish, with its shiny walls and its confusion of savoury brown and yellow meats, and its bay leaves, and its wine, and thought, This will celebrate the occasion…

'It is a triumph,' said Mr Bankes, laying his knife down for a moment. He had eaten attentively. It was rich; it was tender. It was perfectly cooked. How did she manage these things in the depths of the country? he asked her. She was a wonderful woman. All his love, all his reverence had returned; and she knew it.

VIRGINIA WOOLF, *TO THE LIGHTHOUSE*, 1927

MAKING THE SUNDAY ROAST LAST THE WEEK
Hot on Sunday,
Cold on Monday,
Hashed on Tuesday,
Minced on Wednesday,
Curried Thursday,
Broth on Friday,
Cottage pie Saturday.

TRADITIONAL

'Roast beef medium' is not only a food. It's a philosophy.

EDNA FERBER, 1887–1968

ANY PART OF PIGGY

Any part of piggy
Is quite all right with me
Ham from Westphalia, ham from Parma
Ham as lean as the Dalai Lama
Ham from Virginia, ham from York,
Trotters, sausages, hot roast pork.
Crackling crisp for my teeth to grind on
Bacon with or without the rind on
Though humanitarian
I'm not a vegetarian.
I'm neither crank nor prude nor prig
And though it may sound infra dig
Any part of darling pig
Is perfectly fine with me.

NOËL COWARD, *NOT YET THE DODO*, 1967

ERMINTRUDE

Aunt Ermintrude, a prudish type,
Yelled, 'Come on, Malcolm! Eat your tripe!
You say you'd rather have dessert?
This IS dessert, you little squirt!'

Aunt Ermintrude, you may conclude,
Imbued her brood with ghastly food
Like lard and spinach, tripe and such
(The things which sane folk never touch).

Young Malcolm, whose revenge was swift,
Gave Ermintrude a birthday gift,
A box of chocolates, soft and hard,
Inside them, spinach, tripe and lard.

Now Aunt agrees, though tripe is cheap,
It's better left inside the sheep.

DOUG MACLEOD

OVER-INDULGENCE

One day a great feast was held, and after dinner the representation of Solomon, his Temple and the coming of the Queen of Sheba was made, or, as I may better say, was meant to have been made, before their Majesties, by device of the Earl of Salisbury and others. But alas! as all earthly things do fail to poor mortals in enjoyment, so did prove our presentment hereof. The Lady who did play the Queen's part did carry most precious gifts to both their Majesties; but forgetting the steppes arising to the canopy, overset her caskets into his Danish Majesties lap, and fell at his feet, tho I rather think it was in his face. Much was the hurry and confusion; cloths and napkins were at hand to make all clean. His Majesty then got up and would dance with the Queen of Sheba; but he fell down and humbled himself before her, and was carried to an inner chamber and laid on a bed of state; which was not a little defiled with the presents of the Queen which had been bestowed upon his garments; such as wine, cream, jelly, beverage, cakes, spices and other good matters. The entertainment and shew went forward and most of the presenters went backwards, or fell down, wine did so occupy their upper chambers. Now did appear in rich dress, Hope, Faith and Charity: Hope did assay to speak, but wine rendered her endeavours so feeble that she withdrew, and hoped the King would excuse her brevity. Faith was then all alone, for I am certain she was not joyned with good works; and left the Court in a staggering condition. Charity came to the Kings feet, and seemed to cover the multitude of sins her sister had committed: In some sorte she made obeysance and bought giftes, but said she would return home again, as there was no gift which Heaven had not already given his Majesty; she then returned to Hope and Faith, who were both sick and spewing in the lower hall. Next came *Victory*, in bright armour, and prsented a rich sword to the King, who did not accept it, but put it by with his hand; and buy a strange medley of versification, did endeavour to make suit to the King; but Victory did not triumph for long for, after much much lamentable utterance, she was led away like a silly captive, and laid to sleep in the outer steps of the anti-chamber. Now did Peace make entry, and strive to get foremoste to the King; but I grieve to tell how great wrath she did discover unto those of her attendants, and, much contrary to her own semblance, most rudely made war with her olive branch, and laid on the pates of those who did oppose her coming. I have much marvelled at these strange pageantries, and they do bring to my remembrance what passed of this sort in our Queens days: of which I was sometime an humble presenter and assistant; but I ne'er did see such lack of good order, discretion and sobriety...

SIR JOHN HARRINGTON, 1606

It is, of course, true that we can be intemperate in eating as well as in drinking, but the results of the intemperance would appear to be different. After a fifth helping of rice-pudding one does not become over-familiar with strangers, nor does an extra slice of ham inspire a man to beat his wife. After five pints of beer (or fifteen, or fifty) a man 'will go anywhere in reason, but he won't go home'; after five helps of rice-pudding, I imagine, home would seem to him the one-desired haven. The two intemperances may be equally blameworthy, but they are not equally offensive to the community. Yet for some reason over-eating is considered the mark of the beast, and over-drinking the mark of rather a fine fellow.

The poets and other gentlemen who have written so much romantic nonsense about 'good red wine' and 'good brown ale' are responsible for this. I admit that a glass of Burgundy is a more beautiful thing than a blancmange, but I do not think that it follows that a surfeit of one is more heroic than a surfeit of the other... If only the poets had praised over-eating rather than over-drinking, how much pleasanter the streets would be on festival nights!

A. A. MILNE, *NOT THAT IT MATTERS*, 1882–1956

165

28 April 1764

It gave me great concern that you had been in distress, but did not appear strange; the change from an idle dissipated life to a life of application and study was so great that it could not but affect your spirits. I remember Dr Cheyne, a physician at Bath, having, by too full living, brought himself to that degree of corpulency that he had his coach made to open wholly on the side and was really become a burden to himself, resolved to live abstemiously, and reduced his body so much that he was obliged to be swaddled to make his loose skin clasp to his body. By this operation his intellectuals were reduced prodigiously and his spirits sunk to the greatest degree. However, as he had given a strict charge to his friends to keep him at it, by degrees he became inured to the new way of living and all his faculties, with his spirits, returned.

LORD AUCHINLECK, LETTER TO HIS SON JAMES BOSWELL,

WHO WAS STUDYING LAW AT UTRECHT

Gluttony is, I think, less common among women than among men. Women commonly eat more sparingly, and are less curious in the choice of meat; but if once you find a woman gluttonous, expect from her very little virtue. Her mind is enslaved to the lowest and grossest temptation.

DR JOHNSON IN JAMES BOSWELL, *LIFE OF SAMUEL JOHNSON*, 1791

---

20 February 1870

Drunk too much port after dinner at Cae Mawr last night and a splitting headache all day today in revenge. Eyes better but not much. Everything in a daze and dazzle and I could hardly see to read. Got through the services somehow, but in the afternoon came to a deadlock in the 1st Lesson. A blessed change in the weather. Wind westerly and no longer deadly poison.

FRANCIS KILVERT, *DIARY*, 1870-79

Lady seated next to Anthony Trollope:

'You seem to have a good appetite, Mr Trollope.'

Trollope:

'Not at all, Madam, but, thank God, I am very greedy.'

(ATTRIBUTED)

What actually constitutes over-indulgence is very much a matter of what you're used to. These days we tend to be a bit Puritan about some of the good things in life. Not so in bygone days. When I was reading the biography of theatrical impresario George Edwardes I came across the following description of the eating habits of a comfortably well-off family in the latter years of the nineteenth century. Edwardes, known to his company as 'the Guv'nor', ran the Gaiety Theatre, famous for its beautiful chorus girls 'The Gaiety Girls' – many of whom captured a rich or aristocratic husband out of the audience. The housekeeping habits of the newly married Mrs Edwardes were clearly not influenced by fear of putting on weight.

They lived magnificently, and ate so much that we today are flabber-gasted by the mere thought of it. Breakfast was a voluminous meal, the like of which we shall never see again. The handsome sideboard was set out as a high altar for sacrament, and laden with luxurious dishes of all kinds. The strong smell of meths dominated everything, for the gallant silver spirit lamps were arranged under each dish to keep the contents deliciously hot. There were grilled kidneys with pink curls of bacon; fried soles furry with breadcrumbs; steak for Papa, who being the head of the house required fortification; fried eggs, boiled eggs, omelettes plain and assorted; no limit to the richness and variety of the menu. Coffee was not the fashion because rumour had it that 'it did something to the inside', nobody being definite as to what that something was. But tea was very noticeably present in a pregnant-looking pot of solid sil-ver monogrammed and embossed. Only the less fortunate dared flaunt their food and tea in Britannia metal!

A couple of earnest maidservants hovered in the background to attend to needs, unless of course the family happened to be in the better class, when naturally there were footmen to attend to all requirements.

Lunch was an ample meal of soup, fish, and roast, with several lus-cious puddings, copious cheeses and fruits. It was enlivened by the accompaniment of marsala and madeira, and a great deal of good port which was reputed to make blood. Incidentally the port had put in a welcome pre-lunch appearance about eleven o'clock, with a tempting companion in the form of a silver biscuit barrel containing macaroons to sustain the strength. It was vitally important to eat. The strength must be fortified at all costs, and frequently. A good appetite was admired, save in a young lady, when it was considered to be indelicate. Young ladies languished and aspired to the eighteen-inch waist. Young ladies were never hungry!

Tea was a five o'clock meal served on a crochet cloth with a pre-dominant silver muffin-dish. There were Sally Lunns, crumpets and pikelets; cucumber sandwiches, jam sandwiches, Gentleman's Relish sandwiches; and raw beef sandwiches for the males (considerable atten-tion being devoted to the necessary business of propping up masculine strength). There was a plum cake and seed cake, iced cake and parkin, but no pastries or cream cakes. One ate pastries in France, Mamma would mention with some contempt, for she was having nothing of that sort in *her* home!

But dinner was the great meal.

This could never be hurried. A dressing gong was sounded half an hour previously, and the next gong could not be clashed until everybody had gathered together, for there must be no danger of good food cooling, though I should have thought this to be highly improbable seeing the enormous silver meat covers which bellied over all dishes and added much to the pomposity of the side tables...

As though one had not had enough, last thing at night a tray appeared with a variety of tempting sandwiches, cakes, patties and such, to prevent night starvation.

URSULA BLOOM, *CURTAIN CALL FOR THE GUV'NOR*, 1954

——◆——

Enclosing every thin man, there's a fat man demanding elbow-room.

EVELYN WAUGH, *OFFICERS AND GENTLEMEN*, 1955

——◆——

Gluttony is an emotional escape, a sign something is eating *us*.

PETER DE VRIES, *COMFORT ME WITH APPLES*, 1956

——◆——

PLAINT OF A PERVERSE PALATE
I have dined too long off delicate food:
I am now in far too coarse a mood:
Bring me a thick beefsteak *saignant*,
A mountain of cheese and an onion,
Garlic soup and a smoking mess
Of fish unknown to *bouillabaisse*!
My palate is perversely off
Dinde truffée, sauce Stroganoff.

Suprème and Mornay and Cardinal,
Dubarry and Hollandaise *et al*,
Give me coarse black bread and boeuf tartare,
I am sick to death of caviar.

I have drunk too deep of delicate wine
To broach a bottle of Rieselstein,
Hospices de Beaune or Gruaud Larose,
Nuits-St-Georges or any château's
Ancient and throat caressing *cru*:
I thirst for some far stronger brew.
The fierce and brutal joys I seek
Of planter's run, from Martinique,
Grappa and vodka and arrack,
Eau de vie and applejack.
I am bored with cocktails at the Ritz:
Bring me a bottle of slivovitz!

GEORGE SLOCOMBE

170

The trouble with me is that I just enjoy more and more things,' said
Emma. 'First I just liked milk; then I learned to like tea and coffee, and
then cocoa and lemonade; and then port and sherry; and then gin and
whisky. Soon I shall like everything.'

MALCOLM BRADBURY, *EATING PEOPLE IS WRONG*

A wonderful bird is the pelican,
His bill will hold more than his belican.
He can take in his beak food enough for a week,
But I'm damned if I see how the helican.

D. L. MERRITT

GREEDYGUTS

I sat in the café and sipped at a Coke.
There sat down beside me a WHOPPING great bloke
Who sighed as he elbowed me into the wall:
'Your trouble, my boy, is your belly's too small!
Your bottom's too thin! Take a lesson from me:
I may not be nice, but I'm GREAT, you'll agree,
And I've lasted a lifetime by playing this hunch:
The bigger the breakfast, the larger the lunch!

The larger the lunch, then the huger the supper.
The deeper the teapot, the vaster the cupper.
The fatter the sausage, the fuller the tea.
The MORE on the table, the BETTER for ME!'

His elbows moved in and his elbows moved out,
His belly grew bigger, chins wobbled about,
As forkful by forkful and plate after plate,
He ate and he ate and he ate and he ATE!

171

I hardly could breathe, I was squashed out of shape,
So under the table I made my escape.
'Aha!' he rejoiced, 'when it's come to the test,
The fellow who's fattest will come off the best!
Remember, my boy, when it comes to the crunch:
The bigger the breakfast, the larger the lunch!

The larger the lunch, then the huger the supper.
The deeper the teapot, the vaster the cupper.
The fatter the sausage, the fuller the tea.
The MORE on the table, the BETTER for ME!'

A lady came by who was scrubbing the floor
With a mop and a bucket. To even the score,
I lifted that bucket of water and said,
As I poured the whole lot of it over his head:

'*I've* found all my life, it's a pretty sure bet:
The FULLER the bucket, the WETTER you GET!'

KIT WRIGHT, 1981

PICNICS AND FOOD
FOR TRAVELLERS

Many years ago a young actor was hobbling along a dusty road in company with a very old actor, when they passed a party of people enjoying a picnic by the side of the lane. A large Rolls-Royce was parked nearby. Two tables had been set out with fine linen, silver, and crystal glasses. Vintage wine was being uncorked, and delicious food was being served by the butler.

'Oh look, sir!' said the young actor. 'How marvellous it would be to live like that.'

'Never mind, laddie,' said the old actor. 'They may have a Rolls-Royce, plenty of money and fine clothes. They may have crystal glasses and vintage wines and live in luxury; but remember one thing my boy… THEY CANNOT ACT!'

We both adore that anecdote, which was a favourite in the repertoire of the actor Geoffrey Lumsden. Geoffrey loved actors and acting and for him *proper* acting meant just one thing: STAGE acting.

The tale is a wonderful reminder of how, for so many actors, people and events outside their profession are of almost no interest. There is a story – apocryphal we're sure – that on the morning the Second World War was headlined in all the newspapers Sir John Gielgud, coming down for breakfast and hearing everyone talking about the major calamity that had befallen, assumed they were talking about the bad notices in the papers for an actress friend's first night!

This cavalier attitude to the rest of the world is combined, paradoxically, with an enormous generosity of spirit that makes people willing to perform for nothing in a never-ending sequence of charity galas. It was beautifully summed up by Noël Coward, the epitome of the profession, in one of his many songs:

> We're going to do a Midnight Matinée!
> We're going to do a Midnight Show!
> We're not quite sure
> What charity it's for
> But probably the Press will know…

> 'Ay, heave the ballast overboard,
> And stow the eatables in the aft locker.'
> 'Would not this keg be best a little lowered?'
> 'No; now all's right.' 'Those bottles of warm tea –
> (Give me some straw) – must be stowed tenderly;
> Such as we used, in summer after six,
> To cram in greatcoat pockets, and to mix
> Hard eggs and radishes and rolls at Eton.
> And, couched on stolen hay in those green harbours
> Farmers called gaps, and we schoolboys called arbours,
> Would feast till eight.'

PERCY BYSSHE SHELLEY, *BOAT ON THE SERCHIO*, 1822

> Lemonade
> Made in the shade
> Stirred with a spade
> By an old maid.

TRADITIONAL

One of the pleasantest forms of entertainment is a well-arranged picnic (if only a fine day be selected), while nothing is calculated to give greater dissatisfaction than a badly-managed one. To have chosen the wrong people (even one or two, who are likely not to make themselves agreeable), to have given people wrong seats in the various vehicles, or to have too many ladies in the party, are all often fatal errors.

We say nothing of the mistakes made about the luncheon or dinner, when, as is often the case, the ladies provide this, each taking what she likes, with the result, that there is too much of one thing and too little of another: plenty of salad and no dressing; two or three legs of lamb and no mint sauce; an abundance of wine and no corkscrew; and such like little accidents. Given a happy party of young people bent on enjoyment, these are trifles light as air, which serve rather to increase the fun than diminish it. But on the other hand, the party may not all be young and merry; it may be very distasteful to some to have to eat meat without *bread*, and almost impossible without *salt*, while no corkscrew being at hand, it will rouse their indignation to see the necks of bottles knocked off, or the corks incompletely picked out with a penknife; and yet, in the annals of picnics, all these things, bread, salt and corkscrew have been forgotten.

The easiest way to arrange that there should be nothing wanting, if the ladies provide the repast, is for one lady (the most competent) to make out a menu, adding all the little etceteras, and apportion to each one her share.

The following menus for picnics may be found useful, the prices and quantities being given; while a list of requirements, in addition to the viands, will be found at the foot.

PICNIC LUNCHEON FOR TWENTY PERSONS – SUMMER					
No. 1	Average Cost		No.2	Average Cost	
	s.	d.		s.	d.
5 lbs. of Cold Salmon.	7	6	4 Lobsters.	10	0
Mayonnaise Sauce.	1	0	8 lbs. of Cold Boiled Beet.	6	10
1 Quarter of Lamb.	10	0	2 Veal Pies.	7	0
Mint Sauce.	0	4	3 Roast Fowls.	7	6
1 Large Galantine of Veal.	7	6	1 Tongue.	3	6
3 Boiled Chickens.	7	6	Salad.	2	0
1 Ham.	8	0	Dressing.	0	6
2 Pigeon Pies.	9	0	2 lbs. of Tomatoes	1	6
Salad. Dressing.	2	6	2 Fruit Tarts. Custard.	4	6
2 Cucumbers.	1	0	1 Lemon Sponge.	1	6
2 Fruit Tarts.	3	6	Cheesecakes	2	0
Pastry Sandwiches.	2	0	2 Jellies.	5	0
2 Jellies. 2 Creams.	11	6	2 Creams.	5	0
Custard	1	0	1 Gallon of Strawberries.	4	0
1 Gallon of Strawberries.	4	0	4 lbs. of Cherries.	2	0
3 lbs. of Grapes.	6	0	1lb. of Cheese.	1	0
1 lb. of Cheese	1	0	½ lb. of Butter.	0	9
½ lb. of Butter.	0	9	4 loaves of Bread, or Rolls	1	0
4 loaves of Bread, or Rolls	1	0	1 lb. of Biscuits	0	6
	4 5	1		3 6	1

Wines, bottled beer, soda water, lemonade. Plates, knives, forks, spoons, glasses, tumblers, tablecloth, serviettes, glass cloths, pepper, cayenne, salt, mustard, oil, vinegar, castor sugar, corkscrews and champagne-opener.

MRS BEETON, *MRS BEETON'S BOOK OF HOUSEHOLD MANAGEMENT*, 1861

Here with a Loaf of Bread beneath the Bough,
A Flask of Wine, a Book of Verse – and Thou
Beside me singing in the Wilderness –
And Wilderness is paradise enow.

EDWARD FITZGERALD, *THE RUBÁIYÁT OF OMAR KHAYYÁM*, 1859

A picnic should be held among green things. Green turf is absolutely an essential... There should certainly be hills and dales... and, above all, there should be running water.

ANTHONY TROLLOPE, *CAN YOU FORGIVE HER?*, 1864

'Look here! If you've really nothing else on hand this morning, supposing we drop down the river together, and have a long day of it?'

The Mole waggled his toes from sheer happiness, spread his chest with a sigh full of contentment, and leaned back blissfully into the soft cushions. '*What* a day I'm having!' he said. 'Let us start at once!'

'Hold hard a minute, then!' said the Rat. He looped the painter through a ring in his landing-stage, climbed up into his hole above, and after a short interval reappeared staggering under a fat, wicker luncheon basket.

'Shove that under your feet,' he observed to the Mole, as he passed it down into the boat. Then he untied the painter and took the sculls again.

'What's inside it?' asked the Mole, wriggling with curiosity.

'There's cold chicken inside it,' replied the Rat briefly; 'coldtongue coldhamcoldbeefpickledgerkinssaladfrenchrollscresssandwidges pottedmeatgingerbeerlemonadesodawater– '

'O stop, stop,' cried the Mole in ecstasies: 'This is too much!'

'Do you really think so?' inquired the Rat seriously. 'It's only what I always take on these little excursions; and the other animals are always telling me that I'm a mean beast and cut it *very* fine!'

KENNETH GRAHAME, *THE WIND IN THE WILLOWS*, 1908

The only acceptable British circumstance for a picnic, as far as I'm concerned, is whelks with vinegar and pepper in the car parked on the sea front somewhere, with headscarves on and the windows rolled down.

JEREMY ROUND, *THE INDEPENDENT COOK*, 1988

It is all stuff that you hear about eating and drinking plentifully inducing fever etc., etc., during a long journey. Eating and drinking copiously produce nothing, mind and body being well regulated, but sleepiness – and I know no place where that inclination may be indulged less reprehensibly than in a mail-coach, for at least sixteen hours out of the four-and-twenty. In travelling, I make a point to eat whenever I can sit down, and to drink (ale) whenever the coach stops. As for the interim, when I can neither eat nor drink, I smoke if upon deck, and snuff inside.

N.B. Of course, I mean when there is no opportunity of flirtation.

WILLIAM MAGINN, *MAXIMS OF SIR WILLIAM O'DOHERTY, BART.*, 1849

We are often told in our newspapers that England is disgraced by this and by that; by the unreadiness of our army, by the unfitness of our navy, by the irrationality of our laws, by the immobility of our prejudices, and what not; but the real disgrace of England is the railway sandwich, that whited sepulchre, fair enough outside, but so meagre, poor and spiritless within, such a thing of shreds and parings, such a dab of food, telling us that the poor bone, whence it was scraped, had been made utterly bare before it was sent into the kitchen for the soup pot.

ANTHONY TROLLOPE, *HE KNEW HE WAS RIGHT*, 1869

PUDDINGS

Blessed be he that invented the pudding, for it is a Manna that hits the palates of all sorts of People. A manna better than that of the Wildreness, because the people are never weary of it. Ah, what an excellent thing is an English Pudding! To come in Pudding Time, is as much as to say, to come in the most lucky Moment in the World.

MONSIEUR MISSION, EARLY EIGHTEENTH CENTURY

When our daughters, Kate and Lucy, lived at home I always diligently cooked a proper main course for the evening meal, and during Lucy's vegetarian bouts I cooked two main courses. Not aspiring to the Mother of the Year award, I rarely got round to making a pudding as well. So every evening I would ask if anyone would like yoghurt, fruit or ice-cream. This became such a family ritual that even now, when the girls come for a meal and I start to say, 'Now, for pudding…' they chime in with the time-honoured list plus endless variations on a theme: fruit yoghurt, yoghurt ice-cream, ice-cream with fruit, fruit-flavoured ice-cream etc., etc. Puddings have therefore become something of a challenge, and I have become something of an expert at recipes that are interesting but take little longer than scooping out a tub of ice-cream.

One such favourite is Creole Bananas, my version of a recipe I found in a cookery book by Jocasta Innes more than twenty years ago.

180

CREOLE BANANAS
2 bananas per person (they shrink when cooked and
most people can manage 2)
raisins and/or sultanas
a little lemon zest and orange zest
juice of 2 oranges and ½ lemon
1 tablespoon rum or brandy
butter or margarine

Peel the bananas then slice them in half lengthways and arrange on a buttered ovenproof dish. Sprinkle them with a handful of raisins or sultanas and the lemon and orange zest. Mix the orange and lemon juice with the rum or brandy and pour over the fruit. Dot with butter or margarine and bake, uncovered, in a medium oven – 180–190°C (350–375°F) gas mark 4–5 – for 15–20 minutes, until the bananas are soft but not mushy and the liquid has reduced a little. Serve piping hot with whipped cream.

A delicious variation at Christmas is to dot the fruit with any leftover brandy butter instead of the plain sort. In this case use more lemon juice to counteract the sweetness of the brandy butter and adjust the amount of brandy in the sauce to taste.

'I'll not listen to reason,' she said, now in full possession of her voice, which had been rather choked with sobbing. 'Reason always means what some one else has got to say. Now I think what I've got to say is good enough reason. But, reason or not, I'll say it, and I'll stick to it. I've money in the Savings Bank, and I've a good stock of clothes, and I'm not going to leave Miss Matty. No! not if she gives me warning every hour of the day!'

She put her arms akimbo, as much as to say she defied me; and, indeed, I could hardly tell how to begin to remonstrate with her, so much did I feel that Miss Matty, in her increasing infirmity, needed the attendance of this kind and faithful woman.

'Well!' said I at last –

'I'm thankful you begin with "well!" If you'd ha' begun with "but", as you did afore, I'd not ha' listened to you. Now you may go on.'

'I know you would be a great loss to Miss Matty, Martha – '

'I told her so. A loss she'd never cease to be sorry for,' broke in Martha, triumphantly.

'Still, she will have so little – so very little – to live upon, that I don't see just now how she could find you food – she will even be pressed for her own. I tell you this, Martha, because I feel you are like a friend to dear Miss Matty, but you know she might not like to have it spoken about.'

Apparently this was even a blacker view of the subject than Miss Matty had presented to her; for Martha just sat down on the first chair that came to hand, and cried out loud – (we had been standing in the kitchen).

At last she put her apron down, and looking at me earnestly in the face, asked, 'Was that the reason Miss Matty wouldn't order a pudding today? She said she had no fancy for sweet things, and you and she would just have a mutton-chop. But I'll be up to her. Never you tell, but I'll make her a pudding, and a pudding she'll like, too, and I'll pay for it myself; so mind you see she eats it. Many a one has been comforted in their sorrow by seeing a good dish come upon the table.'

MRS GASKELL, *CRANFORD*, 1853

———

It's funny the way that so many simple pleasures, which should remain uncomplicated, can quickly become hedged about with what, for want of a better word, we have to refer to as snobbery. There is such a fine line between snobbery, which is designed to make you feel terrible, and etiquette, which is designed to guide you effortlessly through social encounters. But snobbery is not as pernicious, or certainly not as obvious, as it was forty or fifty years ago. In those days even a simple pudding could create a social minefield...

182

Mr Fulton has never in all his life, so he says, boiled an egg. 'I arrange my life, and always have done,' he explains, 'so that other people shall boil my eggs for me.' All the same, Mr Fulton likes to discourse on food, and he is very fussy about it. 'But my dear mother,' he told Gwen the other day, 'was always agitating herself about what we should have. Women always make so much out of these small things. My mother used frequently to say when I was a boy, "Whatever can we have for a pudding today?"' He cocked an eyebrow at Gwen. 'Sweet, I daresay she said. But not afters... "Afters" – a most repulsive expression, isn't it? I have heard it used sometimes by people on buses. People on buses speak in a very common way I have noticed.' He sighed. 'I do not care for my fellow creatures, I am afraid; there are far too many of them.' But Gwen wished to hear more about Mr Fulton's mother. 'Did she make the pudding herself every day?' she asked him. Gwen was enquiring with interest, for Mr Fulton is always most grand about his childhood days, though Mrs Owen is rather apt to give the game away sometimes and disclose facts that show that she and Mr Fulton are not descended from half the earls in England as Mr Fulton would have us believe.

'Sometimes my mother made it herself,' he said, and added quickly, 'for a hobby, you know.' Gwen nodded understandingly.

JONQUIL ANTONY, *MRS DALE AT HOME*, 1952

At the end of the meal appeared a rum jelly. This was the Prince's favourite pudding, and the Princess had been careful to order it early that morning in gratitude for favours granted. It was rather threatening at first sight, shaped like a tower with bastions and battlements and smooth slippery walls impossible to scale, garrisoned by red and green cherries and pistachio nuts; but into its transparent and quivering flanks a spoon plunged with astounding ease. By the time the amber-coloured fortress reached Francesco Paolo, the sixteen-year-old son who was served last, it consisted only of shattered walls and hunks of wobbly rubble. Exhilarated by the aroma of rum and the delicate flavour of the multi-coloured garrison, the Prince enjoyed watching the rapid demolishing of the fortress beneath the assault of his family's appetite. One of his glasses was half-full of Marsala. He raised it, glanced round the family, gazed for a second into Concetta's blue eyes, then said; 'To the health of our Tancredi.' He drained his wine in a single gulp. The initials F. D., which had stood out clearly on the golden colour of the full glass, were no longer visible.

GIUSEPPE DI LAMPEDUSA, *THE LEOPARD*, 1958

SALADS

RECIPE FOR A SALAD

To make this condiment your poet begs
The pounded yellow of two hard-boil'd eggs;
Two boiled potatoes, passed through kitchen sieve,
 Smoothness and softness to the salad give.
 Let onion atoms lurk within the bowl,
  And, half-suspected, animate the whole.
 Of mordant mustard add a single spoon,
 Distrust the condiment that bites so soon;
  But deem it not, thou man of herbs, a fault
 To add a double quantity of salt;
Four times the spoon with oil of Lucca crown,
And twice with vinegar procur'd from town;
And lastly o'er the flavour'd compound toss
A magic soupçon of anchovy sauce.
Oh, green and glorious! Oh, herbaceous treat!
Twould tempt the dying anchorite to eat;
Back to the world he'd turn his fleeting soul,
And plunge his fingers in the salad bowl!
Serenely full, the epicure would say,
'Fate cannot harm me, I have dined today.'

SYDNEY SMITH, 1771–1845

For a good salad be a spendthrift for oil, a miser for vinegar, a statesman for salt, and a madman for mixing.

SPANISH PROVERB

To make a good salad is to be a brilliant diplomatist – the problem is entirely the same in both cases. To know exactly how much oil one must put with one's vinegar.

OSCAR WILDE, *VERA, OR THE NIHILISTS*, 1880

Soliloquy of a Tortoise
on Revisiting
the Lettuce Beds
after an Interval of one Hour
while supposed
to be
Sleeping
in a Clump
of Blue Hollyhocks

One cannot have enough
Of this delicious stuff!

E. V. RIEU

SELF-SUFFICIENCY

S elf-sufficiency inevitably brings me round to the subject of *The Good Life*, the television series that I did in the 1970s with three actors who have become firm friends: Felicity Kendal (playing my wife, Barbara Good), Penelope Keith and Paul Eddington (playing our neighbours, Margo and Jerry Leadbetter). The title combined a pun on my character's name – Tom Good – with the idea of a simple 'good' life of self-sufficiency, albeit in suburban Surbiton. The scripts by John Esmonde and Bob Larbey were absolute crackers, and the idea of self-sufficiency seemed to tap into a hidden yearning in the television audience at a time when everything around us was becoming increasingly materialistic. Doing the show hardly seemed like work at all: I loved every minute. But I have always had a special spot in my heart for the very first episode, when Tom Good, unfulfilled head of an advertising agency's design stu-

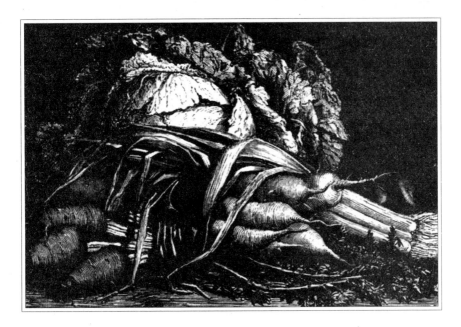

dio, reaches a mid-life crisis on his fortieth birthday. Can he spend the next twenty-five years thinking up silly promotional ideas to sell more packets of cereal? No, he cannot. A new life, a better life, a life close to nature and to the soil of his own back garden is calling him...

There was an expression of sheer excitement on Tom's face.

'Listen, Barbara, you know that "It" business? I've finally defined what "It" is. It's breaking the circle.'

'What circle?'

'Going to work to get money to convert into things which you use up, which makes you go to work again etc., etc.,... the norm. What we should be doing is working at the job of living itself.'

Barbara blinked.

'Is this some sort of religious conversion?' she asked.

'Yes, it is.'

Tom's excitement mounted as he paced back and forth.

'This is it in practical terms. I quit work and we become as damn near self-sufficient as possible. We've got bags of garden. We grow our own food. We keep some animals – some chickens, a pig – produce our own energy, recycle rubbish. We design things we need – I'll show you what being a designer is all about. Some things we can't make – right. Some things we can't grow – right. So we flog our surplus and buy stuff. And that's without good old-fashioned medieval barter. It'll be bloody hard work and we won't have much in the way of mod. cons. but we might even enjoy discovering what we *can* do without. But we won't need the world and his wife to give us the yea or nay. It will be just us – doing it for us. What do you think?'

JOHN ESMONDE AND BOB LARBEY, *THE GOOD LIFE*, 1976

The idea of self-sufficiency is hardly new: part of its appeal is that it harks back to a simpler and less stressful existence. Annie discovered this charming extract from the diary of one of England's greatest artists, John Constable. The diary entry illustrates delightfully the sense of achievement that self-sufficiency brings.

September 16th 1825

This morning, a grand epoch, was ushered in by a prodigious bustle with the fowls in the garden; the black hen making a great to do, the cock strutting about, and Billy [a cat] looking at them in great astonishment from the back kitchen window. When all was a little quiet, I looked into the brewhouse, and saw her on the nest I had made, and at breakfast Elizabeth brought me a beautiful egg, probably the first ever laid in these premises.

EXTRACT FROM JOHN CONSTABLE'S DIARY, IN *MEMOIRS OF THE LIFE OF
JOHN CONSTABLE R.A.* BY CHARLES ROBERT LESLIE R.A.

I'm a keen reader of the lives of my eminent predecessors in the acting profession and no autobiography has given me more pleasure than that of Dame Ellen Terry. From a theatrical family (Sir John Gielgud is one of the dynasty) she became one of the greatest actresses of the nineteenth century as Irving's leading lady at the Lyceum Theatre. But early in her career this unconventional free spirit took several years off to live with her lover, Edward Godwin, and their two children, in the heart of rural Hertfordshire. The following extracts give a good flavour of what her life was like during that idyllic sabbatical.

My hour of rising at this pleasant place near Mackery End in Hertfordshire was six. Then I washed the babies. I had a perfect mania for *washing* everything and everybody...

After the washing I fed the animals. There were two hundred ducks and fowls to feed, as well as the children. By the time I had done this, and cooked the dinner, the morning had flown away. After the midday meal I sewed. Sometimes I drove out in the pony-cart. And in the evening I walked across the common to fetch the milk. The babies used to roam where they liked on this common in charge of a bulldog, while I sat and read.

I studied cookery-books instead of parts – Mrs Beeton instead of Shakespeare.

It was truly the simple life we led in Hertfordshire. From scrubbing floors and lighting fires, cooking, gardening, and harnessing the pony, I grew thinner than ever – as thin as a whipping post, a hurdle, or a haddock!...

We kept a goat, a dear fellow whom I liked very much until I caught him one day chasing my daughter. I seized him by his horns to inflict severe punishment; but then I saw that his eyes were exactly like mine, and it made me laugh so much that I let him go and never punished him at all.

ELLEN TERRY, *THE STORY OF MY LIFE*, 1908

———

I led a most unconventional life, and experienced exquisite delight from the mere fact of being in the country. No one knows what 'the country' means until he or she has lived in it. 'Then, if ever, come perfect days.'

What a sensation it was, too, to be untrammelled by time! Actors must take care of themselves and their voices, husband their strength for the evening's work, and when it is over they are too tired to do anything! For the first time I was able to put all my energies into living. I began gardening, 'the purest of human pleasures'; I learned to cook, and in time cooked very well, though my first essay in that difficult art was rewarded with dire and complete failure.

It was a chicken! Now, as all the chickens had names – Sultan, Duke, Lord Tom Noddy, Lady Teazle, and so forth – and as I was very proud of them as living birds, it was a great wrench to kill one at all, to start with. It was the murder of Sultan, not the killing of a chicken. However, at last it was done, and Sultan deprived of his feathers, floured, and trussed. I had no idea *how* this was all done, but I tried to make him 'sit up' nicely like the chickens in the shops.

He came up to the table looking magnificent – almost turkey-like in his proportions.

'Hasn't this chicken rather an odd smell?' said our visitor.

'How can you!' I answered. 'It must be quite fresh – it's Sultan!'

However, when we began to carve, the smell grew more and more potent.

I had cooked Sultan without taking out his in'ards!

There was no dinner that day except bread-sauce, beautifully made, well-cooked vegetables, and pastry like the foam of the sea. I had a wonderful hand for pastry!

ELLEN TERRY, THE STORY OF MY LIFE, 1908

Richard's admiration for Ellen Terry's self-sufficiency skills, combined with her great acting talent, has not yet persuaded *me* to start growing my own vegetables. However, I do remember one spectacular success in the self-sufficiency stakes enjoyed by a member of my family, although it was more a matter of luck than of judgement.

In 1941 my father dug a deep hole in our back garden and put in an Anderson air-raid shelter, to protect us from enemy bombs. It was lovely and dry in there… until the rain came, whereupon the shelter filled with water. He discovered that it wasn't coming down through the roof or walls but up through the floor, and it turned out that there was an underground stream running through the gardens on our side of the road. So we built an indoor table-shelter instead. The outside one was taken away, the hole was filled in and tomato plants marked the spot where the shelter had been.

The plants loved the well-dug soil and the water coming up from the stream and they produced a wonderful bumper crop of tomatoes. We ate them raw, we ate them cooked, and we gave pounds and pounds of them away. They passed into family history and there never was another crop to match our 'Shelter' tomatoes of the summer of 1941.

STRANGE MEALS

The following recipe, by one of France's most celebrated gourmets, successfully demonstrates the French genius for enjoying the good things of life. Only a Frenchman, surely, could have unselfconsciously compared his meat to his women to the greater glory of both! To be honest, his recipe seems so impossible that I have a sneaky feeling that, like his conquests of the luscious ladies, it may simply be a figment of his imagination.

Stuff an olive with capers and anchovies and put it in a garden warbler. Put the warbler in an ortolan, the ortolan in a lark, the lark in a thrush, the thrush in a quail, the quail in a larded lapwing, the lapwing in a plover, the plover in a red-legged partridge, the partridge in a woodcock – as tender as Mlle Volnais – the woodcock in a teal, the teal in a guinea fowl, the guinea fowl in a duck, the duck in a fattened pullet – as white as Mlle Belmont, as fleshy as Mlle Vienne, as fat as Mlle Contat – the pullet in a pheasant, the pheasant in a large duck, the duck in a turkey – white and fat as Mlle Arsene – and, finally, the turkey in a bustard.

GRIMOD DE LA REYNIÈRE, 1758–1838

We roamed about sweet Sonning for an hour or so, and then, it being too late to push on past Reading, we decided to go back to one of the Shiplake islands, and put up there for the night. It was still early when we got settled, and George said that, as we had plenty of time, it would be a splendid opportunity to try a good slap-up supper. He said he would show us what could be done up the river in the way of cooking, and suggested that, with the vegetables and the remains of the cold beef and general odds and ends, we should make an Irish stew.

It seemed a fascinating idea. George gathered wood and made a fire, and Harris and I started to peel the potatoes. I should never have thought that peeling potatoes was such an undertaking. The job turned out to be the biggest thing of its kind that I had ever been in. We began cheerfully, one might almost say skittishly, but our lightheartedness was gone by the time the first potato was finished. The more we peeled, the more peel there seemed to be left on; by the time we had got all the peel off and all the eyes out, there was no potato left – at least none worth speaking of. George came and had a look at it – it was about the size of a peanut. He said: 'Oh, that won't do! You're wasting them. You must scrape them.'

So we scraped them, and that was harder work than peeling. They are such an extraordinary shape, potatoes – all bumps and warts and hollows. We worked steadily for five-and-twenty minutes, and did four potatoes. Then we struck. We said we should require the rest of the evening for scraping ourselves.

I never saw such a thing as potato-scraping for making a fellow in a mess. It seemed difficult to believe that the potato-scrapings in which Harris and I stood, half-smothered, could have come off four potatoes. It shows you what can be done with economy and care.

George said it was absurd to have only four potatoes in an Irish stew, so we washed half a dozen or so more, and put them in without peeling. We also put in a cabbage and about half a peck of peas. George stirred it all up, and then he said that there seemed to be a lot of room to spare, so we overhauled both the hampers, and picked out all the odds and ends and the remnants, and added them to the stew. There were half a pork pie and a bit of cold boiled bacon left, and we put them in. Then George found half a tin of potted salmon, and he emptied that into the pot.

He said that was the advantage of Irish stew: you got rid of such a lot of things. I fished out a couple of eggs that had got cracked, and we put those in. George said they would thicken the gravy.

I forget the other ingredients, but I know nothing was wasted; and I remember that, towards the end, Montmorency, who had evinced great interest in the proceedings throughout, strolled away with an earnest and thoughtful air, reappearing, a few minutes afterwards, with a dead water-rat in his mouth, which he evidently wished to present as his contribution to the dinner; whether in a sarcastic spirit, or with a general desire to assist, I cannot say.

We had a discussion as to whether the rat should go in or not. Harris said that he thought it would be all right, mixed up with the other things, and that every little helped; but George stood up for precedent. He said he had never heard of water-rats in Irish stew, and he would rather be on the safe side, and not try experiments.

Harris said: 'If you never try a new thing, how can you tell what it's like? It's men such as you that hamper the world's progress. Think of the man who first tried German sausage!'

It was a great success, that Irish stew. I don't think I ever enjoyed a meal more. There was something so fresh and piquant about it. One's palate gets tired of the old hackneyed things: here was a dish with a new flavour, with a taste like nothing else on earth.

And it was nourishing, too. As George said, there was good stuff in it. The peas and potatoes might have been a bit softer, but we all had good teeth, so that did not matter much; and as for the gravy, it was a poem – a little too rich, perhaps, for a weak stomach, but nutritious.

JEROME K. JEROME, *THREE MEN IN A BOAT*, 1889

Man's best friend can suffer from a weak stomach sometimes, as the following extract proves.

6.15. Stalked a kitten in kitchen passage. The other little cowards ran away.

6.20. Things are looking brighter, helped mouse escape from cat.

6.30. Upstairs, past the drawing-room. Door of old Mrs Brown's bedroom open invitingly. I entered. Never been in before. Nothing much

worth having. Ate a few flowers out of a bonnet. Beastly. Then into Miss Brown's room. Very tidy when I entered. Discovered there packet labelled 'High Class Pure Confectionary'. Not bad. Pretty room.

7.00. Down to supper. Ate it, but without much relish. I am off my feed today.

7.15. Ate kittens' supper. But I do wish they would not give them that eternal fish. I am getting sick of it.

7.16. Sick of it in the garden.

7.25. Nasty feeling of lassitude comes over me, with loss of all initiative, so I decide to take things quietly, and lie down by the kitchen fire. Sometimes I think that I am not the dog that I was.

8.00. Hooray! Appetite returning.

8.01. Ravenous.

8.02. Have one of the nicest pieces of coal I have ever come across.

8.05. Nose around the kitchen floor, and glean a bit of onion, an imitation tortoise-shell comb, a shrimp (almost entire), an abominably stale chunk of bread, and about half a yard of capital string. After coal, I think I like string best. The family have noticed what a lot of this I stow away, and it was not a bad idea of young Mr Brown's, the other day, that if I had the end of a piece of string always hanging from my mouth, they could use me as a string-box. Though it is scarcely a matter for joking about. Still, it made me laugh.

WALTER EMANUEL, *A DOG DAY OR THE ANGEL OF THE HOUSE*, 1902

Sir, In view of the publicity you have accorded to Mrs Barrow's letter, I hope that you will spare me some space to say, as an advocate for the consumption of grass-mowings, that I have eaten them regularly for over three years, and off many lawns. The sample I am eating at present comes off a golf green on Mitcham Common. I have never suffered from urticaria or any of the symptoms Mrs Barrow mentions. Nor did any of the many of my horses to which I have fed grass-mowings, freshly cut and cleaned from stones etc. For my own consumption I also wash them well.
Yours faithfully,
J. R. B. Branson

LETTER TO *THE TIMES*, 2 MAY 1940

It's a very odd thing –
As odd as can be –
That whatever Miss T. eats
Turns into Miss T.

WALTER DE LA MARE, *MISS T.*

ALLIGATOR
From Sydney Zoo
An alligator
Was put on board
A flying freighter.
He ate the pilot
And the navigator
Then asked for more
With mashed potato.

SPIKE MILLIGAN, *A BOOK OF MILLIGANIMALS*, 1968

Nigel Dauncey's dairy farm near Yeovil, Somerset, sells a range of meats to make a carnivore's heart glow.

Popular lines include kangaroo, peacock, alligator, crocodile, wild boar and ostrich. But this year his company is offering the ultimate starter – locusts, best served in a stir-fry, possibly covered with tomato relish.

'Orders of peacock, boar and the rest are rising, and maybe some diners will try locust,' said Mr Dauncey. But the insects cost £8.50 for ten, and it could be expensive to ensure guests get a decent mouthful.

Mr Dauncey's supplies come from Yorkshire, where they are 'hibernated permanently' in a fridge. Locusts naturally go to sleep when it gets chilly but, in this case, they never wake up.

Mr Dauncey and his partner, Christina Baskerville, prepare the insects by boiling them for five minutes and then drying them in an oven (an African technique). 'They have quite a nutty flavour by themselves, but the relish helps,' Mr Dauncey said.

Customers include hotels, restaurants and esoteric butchers. Organisers of a medical dinner in Bournemouth have ordered them for unsuspecting doctors before the steak.

The company first stumbled on locusts after a regular customer was seeking supplies of mealie bugs, another African insect fond of millet. Realising that locust recipes were popular in Africa, Mr Dauncey had a vision of the market potential. 'They are very healthy to eat – no worries about excess fat,' he said.

In addition to the dairy cattle, the farm also raises 400 wild boar and supplies peacock from an East Anglian breeder. The birds are slaughtered before they reach full plumage, but a few coloured feathers are packaged with the meat.

Alligator meat comes from farms in Louisiana and crocodile from Zimbabwe. Kangaroo is imported from Australia and ostrich from South Africa (English breeders cannot officially slaughter them yet).

'To be interested in our products, our customers have to be slightly different,' said Mr Dauncey.

ANDREW MORGAN IN THE *OBSERVER*, 20 NOVEMBER 1994

STRAWBERRIES

… Mrs Elton, in all her apparatus of happiness, her large
bonnet and her basket, was very ready to lead the
way in gathering, accepting, or talking – strawberries, and only strawberries, could now
be thought or spoken of. – 'The best fruit
in England – every body's favourite – always
wholesome. – These the finest beds and
finest sorts. – Delightful to gather for one's
self – the only way of really enjoying them.
– Morning decidedly the best time – never
tired – every sort good – hautboy infinitely
superior – no comparison – the others hardly eatable
– hautboys very scarce – Chili preferred – white wood
finest flavour of all – price of strawberries in London – abundance about
Bristol – Maple Grove – cultivation – beds when to be renewed – gardeners thinking exactly different – no general rule – gardeners never to
be put out of their way – delicious fruit – only too rich to be eaten much
of – inferior to cherries – currants more refreshing – only objection to
gathering strawberries the stooping – glaring sun – tired to death – could
bear it no longer – must go and sit in the shade.'

JANE AUSTEN, *EMMA*, 1816

Some people tell you you should not drink claret after strawberries.
They are wrong.

WILLIAM MAGINN, *MAXIMS OF SIR WILLIAM O'DOHERTY, BART.*, 1849

TEA

———◆———

Tea! Where would we be without it? Tea is what makes our world go round, or at least start to go round, at about 7.30 in the morning. Most of us simply bung a teabag in a mug of boiling water, squeeze it round the sides with a teaspoon until the liquid goes dark brown, take it out and sling it in the sink, add milk and swill it down – before rushing out to work. This is what we did until we invited the famous comedy actress Athene Seyler over for tea one day. We very rarely invited legendary actresses to tea, and thought we should show a bit of style by having a choice of teas, both Indian and China.

Athene arrived in her splendour, a very sprightly eighty years old – so sprightly in fact that she lived to be 101! We asked nervously which type of tea she would prefer. 'Both, my dears, as you have them,' she replied. She was absolutely right: it truly is delicious. Three teaspoons of Indian to one of China, with semi-skimmed milk. Really light and refreshing. Since that moment we've never drunk tea any other way.

———◆———

All well-regulated families set apart an hour every morning for tea and bread and butter.

JOSEPH ADDISON, 1711

———◆———

Colley Cibber is not a name that rolls easily off the tongue – he was the son of a Schleswig sculptor – but it is still a name to conjure with in theatrical circles. During his long life (1671–1757) he achieved fame as an actor and dramatist, finally becoming Poet Laureate. His powerbase was the Theatre Royal Drury Lane. Perhaps Cibber's most lasting achievement was his 1700 adaptation of Shakespeare's *Richard III*, to which he added the immortal line, 'A horse, a horse, my king-

dom for a horse', thus ensuring that what is possibly Shakespeare's best-known line is not actually by Shakespeare!

Tea, thou soft, thou sober, sage and venerable drink, thou female tongue-running, smile-sweetening, heart-opening, neck-tipping cordial, to whose glorious insipidity I owe the happiest moment of my life, let me prostrate thus and adore thee.

COLLEY CIBBER, 1671–1757

There is very little art in making good tea; if the water is boiling, and there is no sparing of the fragrant leaf, the beverage will almost invariably be good.

MRS BEETON, *MRS BEETON'S BOOK OF HOUSEHOLD MANAGEMENT*, 1861

A man always dines, let his sorrow be what it may. A woman contents herself with tea, and mitigates her sorrow, we must suppose, by an extra cup.

ANTHONY TROLLOPE, *AN OLD MAN'S LOVE*, 1884

I love to have my tea-cup emptied and filled with gradual pauses, so that time for oblivion may accrue, and no exact record be taken.

ANTHONY TROLLOPE, *NORTH AMERICA*, 1862

Making toast by the fireside,
Nurse fell in the grate and died:
And what makes it ten times worse
All the toast was burnt with Nurse.

HARRY GRAHAM, *RUTHLESS RHYMES FOR HEARTLESS HOMES*, 1899

The American journalist Ella Wheeler Wilcox was one of the most successful poets of her generation, despite the fact that her homely verses attracted derision from intellectuals. We cannot pretend that this poem is great literature, but it does capture the old-fashioned charm and comfort of the kettle singing invitingly on the hob. And anyway, the woman who coined the phrase

Laugh and the world laughs with you;
Weep, and you weep alone

surely deserves to be remembered.

THE KETTLE

There's many a house of grandeur,
With turret, tower and dome,
That knows not peace and comfort,
And does not prove a home.
I do not ask for splendour
To crown my daily lot,
But this I ask – a kitchen
Where the kettle's always hot.

If things are not all shipshape,
I do not fume or fret,
A little clean disorder
Does not my nerves upset.

But *one* thing is essential,
Or seems so to my thought,
And that's a tidy kitchen
Where the kettle's always hot.

In my Aunt Hattie's household,
Though skies outside are drear,
Though times are dark and troubled,
You'll always find good cheer.
And in her quaint old kitchen –
The very homiest spot –
The kettle's always singing,
The water's always hot.

And if you have a headache,
Whate'er the hour may be,
There is no tedious waiting
To get your cup of tea.
I don't know how she does it –
Some magic she has caught –
For the kitchen's cool in summer,
Yet the kettle's always hot.

Oh there's naught else so dreary
In household Kingdom found
As a cold and sullen kettle
That does not make a sound.
And I think that love is lacking
In the hearts in such a spot,
Or the kettle would be singing
And the water would be hot.

ELLA WHEELER WILCOX, 1850–1919

Tea, followed by a bridge-party, was, in summer, the chief manifestation of the spirit of hospitality in Tilling. Mrs Poppit, it is true, had attempted to do something in the way of dinner-parties, but though she was at liberty to give as many dinner-parties as she pleased, nobody else had followed her ostentatious example. Dinner-parties entailed a higher scale of living; Miss Mapp, for one, had accurately counted the cost of having three hungry people to dinner, and found that one such dinner-party was not nearly compensated for, in the way of expense, by being invited to three subsequent dinner-parties by your guests. Voluptuous teas were the rule, after which you really wanted no more than little bits of things, a cup of soup, a slice of cold tart, or a dished-up piece of fish and some toasted cheese. Then, after the excitement of bridge (and bridge was very exciting in Tilling) a jig-saw puzzle or Patience cooled your brain and composed your nerves.

E. F. BENSON, *MISS MAPP*, 1922

VEGETABLES

Our younger daughter, Lucy, has been an on-and-off vegetarian since she was twelve years old, and a full-time vegetarian for the past five years. Occasionally it is possible to persuade her to eat fish but mostly it isn't. Richard's mother and his sister Jane both became vegetarians years ago and other vegetarians in our family include my sister and her husband and one of our nieces. Richard and I sympathize with their views and, although we cannot quite bring ourselves to join them, I often cook vegetarian dishes that we both enjoy. One favourite, inspired by a recipe for squash ragoût by Sophie Grigson, is this squash casserole.

SQUASH CASSEROLE
SERVES 2

1 small squash cut into chunks (I use an acorn squash weighing about 1 lb (450 g), which makes roughly 12 oz (350 g) when peeled and de-seeded. You can use other types of squash or pumpkin.)

1–1½ tablespoons olive oil

1 medium onion, chopped

½ green pepper, chopped

1 garlic clove, finely chopped
1 stick celery, sliced
1 small tin sweetcorn, drained
1 small tin tomatoes, including their juice
1 dessertspoon tomato purée
1 dried red chilli, crumbled
2 tablespoons fresh coriander or parsley, chopped (If fresh herbs are not available subsitute dried marjoram or oregano to taste.)
½ glass dry white wine
vegetable stock or water to cover
seasoning (a pinch of sugar, salt and freshly ground black pepper)

Warm the olive oil in an ovenproof casserole dish. Add the onion, green pepper, garlic and celery and soften over a low heat. Add the squash, stir and cook for a minute or so longer. Add all the remaining ingredients, including the wine. Add vegetable stock or water to just cover the vegetables, season to taste, cover and transfer to the oven. Cook at a very low heat – 110–120°C (225–250°F) gas mark ¼–½ – for up to 3 hours. I got into the habit of cooking this extra slowly so that I could prepare it then leave it to cook if I had to go out. You could cook it more quickly at a higher heat.

Serve with potatoes baked in their jackets (washed, dried, rubbed with butter or soft margarine, sprinkled with salt and wrapped in foil) in the oven at the same time.

Delicious with a glass of wine!

'Tis scarce 100 years since we had cabbages out of Holland, Sir Arthur Ashley, of Wilburg St Giles in Dorsetshire, being the first who planted them in England.

Cabbage is not so greatly magnified by the rest of the doctors, as affording but a gross and melancholy juice. Yet loosening, if moderately boil'd. It is seldom eaten raw, except by the Dutch.

1699

It has been a common saying of physicians in England, that a cucumber should be well sliced, and dressed with pepper and vinegar, and then thrown out, as good for nothing.

DR JOHNSON IN JAMES BOSWELL, *LIFE OF SAMUEL JOHNSON*, 1791

... It is past twelve o'clock Anne and i have not tidied ourselves, done our bed work, or done our lessons and we want to go out to play. We are going to have for dinner Boiled Beef, Turnips, potatoes and apple pudding. The kitchin is in a very untidy state Anne and i have not done our music exercise which consists of b major Tabby said on my putting a pen in her face Ya pitter pottering there instead of pilling a potate. I answered O Dear, O Dear, O Dear I will derectly With that I get up, take a knife and begin pilling. Finished pilling the potates...

EMILY BRONTË, LETTER WRITTEN AGED 7

Gravy and potatoes,
In a good brown pot,
Put them in the oven,
And serve them very hot.

TRADITIONAL

All cooks agree in this opinion
No savoury dish without an onion.

ANON

When push comes to shove I prefer my native food to other countries' fare, but I have to admit that there's still a long way to go when it comes to cooking vegetables *à l'anglaise* (Annie's cooking excepted, of course!).

An old friend and I play golf together about four times a year – I believe in the USA it's known as male-bonding – and on one of these jaunts we thought we'd try the clubhouse lunch. We ordered the dish of the day – cauliflower cheese. A motherly waitress duly arrived and placed a large plate in the centre of the table. Upon the plate resided a slightly grey cauliflower with a teaspoon of melted cheese on top. It was entirely soggy and entirely tasteless, eclipsing anything I had seen in the BBC canteen on a bad day. That will teach me to sneak off and play golf on a working day.

———

Vegetables can be food for the gods, though you may think this an overstatement if you have just had a spell of pot luck in provincial hotels up and down the country, or if, perversely, you throw your mind back to train dining-cars or to the smell that hit you as you passed the open door of a seaside boarding house at lunch time one summer's day. I cannot think how even experienced cooks find it possible to turn nice material into such nasty food.

CONSTANCE SPRY, *COME INTO THE GARDEN, COOK*, 1942

MASHED POTATO – LOVE POEM
If I ever had to choose between you
and a third helping of mashed potato,
(whipped lightly with a fork
not whisked,
and a little pool of butter
melting in the middle...)

I think
I'd choose
the mashed potato

But I'd choose you next.

SIDNEY HODDER

WASHING-UP

————◆————

W e don't have a washing-up machine, so we are often at the sink. Richard plunges in, with willingness and verve, but without much attention to detail. Occasionally, half-clean plates or forks, which still have the odd bit of food caught in between their prongs, have to be sneaked back on to the unwashed pile; and he always forgets to scrub the underneath of the saucepans. He has a very low boredom threshold and, invariably, wanders off, leaving spoons, soapsuds and assorted debris in the bottom of the sink. So I finish washing the spoons, clear out the debris and rinse the suds away, then empty the sink-tidy and wipe down the surfaces.

It's possible that our washing-up techniques are indicative of our characters. Richard is all for the Grand Plan, and doesn't worry if things are vague around the edges, while I am for accuracy and therefore try to get the details right. Perhaps that's because I am the daughter of a lawyer. He was very good at *wiping-up*, a much undervalued accomplishment. He would stand there, whistling under his breath, drying each individual item very carefully, while my mother, having dashed through the washing-up, was already on to some other household task. They were a very good combination. Perhaps couples who want to set up home together should take a washing-up test to see if they are compatible!

Throughout my cooking life I have had two bibles. One was the combined works of Elizabeth David, who transformed my attitude to food. The other was *The Constance Spry Cookery Book*, written with Rosemary Hume. Richard bought me a copy in 1962, and I still use it. In addition to recipes it is packed with fascinating and unexpected titbits of information, including the following words of wisdom on the very subject of washing-up.

The following notes are not intended as an affront to the experienced housewife. They are an offering to the young and perhaps newly married wife to enable her, should she so wish, to 'mug up' the subject privily.

Recently I had the opportunity to see at close quarters one or two of the magnificent silver cisterns and fountains that were used in the eighteenth century for washing the silver in the dining-room. This was done, I learned, while the banquet was still in progress in order that the supply of table silver should be adequate. The cistern or bath for the plates was a huge silver oval about 4 foot 6 long and 3 foot 6 wide. Those I saw stood on low feet, bore elegant designs, and the insides were engraved with the owner's coat of arms…

If it has not been your good fortune to watch a well-trained servant, an old-fashioned butler, or a Victorian maiden aunt performing the task of washing up, it is more than likely you will hold it in poor esteem. Indeed, in the hands of the slovenly it can be an offensively unpleasant affair. There was nothing so about the way a good butler cared for his silver, washing one fork or spoon at a time, laying each piece down on a folded cloth, drying, polishing, and putting away with an almost brooding care for something worth looking after. The washing up of old china cups and saucers which I once witnessed was carried out, as was their custom, by the two charming though faded hostesses: warm soft water in a bowl and a snowy cloth having been brought in by the parlourmaid, with a dignity no whit less than that of her mistresses. Then each beautiful bit of china was replaced in the drawing-room of the lovely old Irish house. These refinements of washing up are, I know, but *souvenirs d'autrefois*…

CONSTANCE SPRY AND ROSEMARY HUME,
THE CONSTANCE SPRY COOKERY BOOK, 1956

What Queen Victoria
Eats and Drinks

Her Majesty's tastes in food are, as I have said before, most simple. A tiny slice of boiled chicken, or a cut from the sirloin, which is sent from London every day and roasted at a special fire in the kitchen, or perhaps a slice of game, which, like the beef for the Queen's use, is cooked apart, form the staple portion of Her Majesty's luncheon. She has a partiality for white soup, which in several varieties is often served to her.

The Queen's breakfasts are even plainer than her luncheons. Fish is always on the table, but eggs on toast, or merely boiled, with dry toast and a small selection of fancy bread, are the usual articles put before the Queen at her first meal. There is no doubt that Her Majesty has a strong weakness for afternoon tea. From her early days in Scotland, when Brown and the other gillies used to boil the kettle in a sheltered corner of the moors while Her Majesty and the young Princesses sketched, the refreshing cup of tea has ever ranked high in the Royal favour.

It is principally to supply the Queen's tea-table that the confectionary cooks are kept busy all the year round at Windsor, for wherever the Court may be there must follow a large supply of cakes. Among the favourites of the Queen which are carefully packed in small tin boxes, and sent to the Court four times a week, are chocolate sponges, wafers of two or three different shapes, *langues de chat*, biscuits and drop cakes of all kinds, tablets, petits fours, princess and rice cakes, pralines, almond sweets, and a large quantity of mixed sweets.

Of the fruit that is produced in such profusion at Frogmore the Queen prefers some highly perfumed grapes of a clear amber colour, but she is reasonably proud of the glorious pineapples and peaches that are grown for her, and frequently eats of the fine fruit the Rothschild family often send her. Among vegetables, Her Majesty confesses to a great weakness for potatoes, which are cooked for her in every conceivable way, and are – in common with all that she eats and drinks – set before her by a very faithful servant, who wears no livery, but in sober black stands by the Queen's side at her meals and assists her to everything...

Of Scotch cookery the Queen has a very great appreciation, and on one occasion, when she was staying (after her widowhood) at Dunkeld with the Duke and Duchess of Atholl, she was loud in her praise of the admirable table kept and most astonished to find that the cook was a Scotch woman. It was here that the Queen first tried 'haggis' and liked it very much...

Although Her Majesty daily sees the rarest vintages served at her table, she has for many years contented herself with a small portion of Scotch whisky, which is distilled expressly for her near Balmoral, at the small distillery of John Begg, and which is carefully mixed by her personal attendant with either Apollinaris, soda, or Lithia water. In one thing, however, the Queen may be said to indulge quite freely, and that is tea. The tea consumed in the Palace costs four shillings a pound, and the Queen drinks the same as everyone else. Whether Her Majesty helps to boil the kettle herself, or whether it is brought to her ready made, she always loves her tea. In the year 1887, when she honoured Sir Reginald Hanson, Bart., then Lord Mayor of London, with her presence at tea at the Mansion House, it was charming to watch her carefully remove her gloves, untie her bonnet strings, and fling them over her shoulders, preparatory to enjoying 'the cup that cheers'. Of coffee Her Majesty is not so very fond, though it is beautifully made by her servants.

THE *PRIVATE* LIFE OF THE *QUEEN* BY *ONE* OF *HER* MAJESTY'S *SERVANTS*, 1897

WHISKY AND GIN

Whisky! A wondrous, volatile substance, not to be recommended to the highly strung male animal. I have seen quite nice little men turn into Mafia bosses after passing the thin red line that separates the end of the second glass and the foolhardy consumption of the third. Annie and I have met only one man who can really handle whisky and that is our oldest friend, the theatre and film director Harold French. He takes it slowly with plenty of water for several hours a day. He has been doing this for about seventy years and is the fittest man of ninety-five we know! Keep going, dear Harold. You are a lesson to us all on the art of whisky drinking without the resulting catastrophes. I haven't the discipline myself so I leave it alone, but not without some regrets.

[Whisky] sloweth age; it strengtheneth youth; it helpeth digestion; it cutteth fleume; it abandoneth melancolie; it relisheth the harte; it lighteneth the mynde; it quickeneth the spirites; it cureth the hydropsie; it healeth the stangury; it pounceth the stone; it repelleth gravel; it puffeth away ventositie; it kepyth and preserveth the hed from whyrling – the eyes from dazelyng – the toungue from lispyng – the mouth from snafflyng – the throat from ratlyng – the weasan from stieflyng – the stomache from wamblyng – the harte from swellyng – the belly from wirtchyng – the guts from rumblyng – the hands from shiveryng – the sinowes from shrinkyng – the veynes from crumplyng – the bones from akyng – the marrow from soakyng... trulie it is a soveraigne liquor.

HOLINSHED, FL. 1577

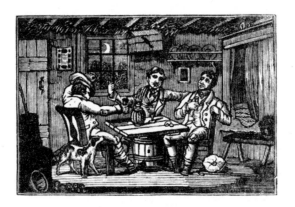

ATHOL BROSE
Charm'd with a drink which Highlanders compose,
A German traveller exclaimed with glee, –
'Potztausend! sare, if dis is Athol Brose,
How goot dere Athol Boetry must be!'

THOMAS HOOD

No man needs be afraid of drinking a very considerable quantity of neat whisky, when in the wilds of Ireland or Scotland. The mountain air requires to be balanced by another stimulus; and if you wish to be really well, you must always take a bumper before you get out of bed, and another before getting into it, according to the fashion of the country you are in.

WILLIAM MAGINN, *MAXIMS OF SIR WILLIAM O'DOHERTY, BART.*, 1849

I was a little exhausted when I arrived [at the War Office] and asked the tall ex-Guards soldier in attendance for a glass of water.
'Certainly, Sir: Irish or Scotch?'

VISCOUNT HALDANE 1856–1928, IN *HALDANE OF CLOAN* BY DUDLEY SOMMER

SLOE GIN

The clear weather of juniper
darkened into winter.
She fed gin to sloes
and sealed the glass container.

When I unscrewed it
I smelled the disturbed
tart stillness of a bush
rising through the pantry.

When I poured it
it had a cutting edge
and flamed
like Betelgeuse.

I drink to you
in smoke-mirled, blue-black,
polished sloes, bitter
and dependable.

SEAMUS HEANEY, *STATION ISLAND*, 1984

WINE

We like drinking wine very much and have, over the years, tried out the offerings of most wine-producing countries, including England. However, practice has not made perfect in our case. Although we can tell the very good from the very bad we gaze with awe at those wine experts who, by delicately sniffing the bouquet, swirling the wine around the glass to get a look at its colour and 'legs', and then gargling the wine over their back teeth (or so it seems to us), are able to give an exact description of the tipple, right down to the very acre on which the vines were grown. When we were young our families didn't drink wine very often, the occasional festive sherry being more in their line, so our lack of expertise may have something to do with being late initiates into the pleasure of wine drinking.

In our early days together, alcohol necessarily came lower on our list of priorities than rent and bread and butter. However, we can recall one incident that indicated that more festive times were to come. During the year in which we met at the Liverpool Playhouse I fell ill, and Annie nobly looked after me. Her mother, thinking that we might be rather 'run down', gave us a bottle of tonic wine. Late one night, when Annie got in from the theatre, we decided to try to build ourselves up with a dose of what we took to be a kind of medicine. I sat up in bed, Annie perched next to me and we both had a small glassful. It certainly gave

us a warm glow, which we assumed was due to its medicinal proper-
ties, so we thought we might try another glass, and then another. Soon
we were overcome by the giggles, which quickly turned to hysteria
when I tried to place my (full) glass down on the bedside shelf and
missed completely. The uninhibited laughter made us feel much better
and ever since that evening we have thoroughly appreciated what a tonic
a glass of wine can be, whatever the name on the label.

A LOGICAL PROGRESSION
Good wine maketh good blood,
Good blood causeth good humours,
Good humours cause good thoughts,
Good thoughts bring forth good works,
Good works carry a man to heaven;
Ergo, Good wine carrieth a man to heaven.

ANON

In drinking claret, when that cold wine begins, as it
will do, to chill the stomach, a glass of brandy, after
every four glasses of claret corrects the frigidity.
WILLIAM MAGINN, *MAXIMS OF SIR WILLIAM
O'DOHERTY, BART.*, 1849

I confess... that I like wine... it seems to me that my
dinner goes down better with a glass of sherry than
without it.
ANTHONY TROLLOPE, *NORTH AMERICA*, 1862

The Germans are exceedingly fond of Rhine wines;
they are put up in tall, slender bottles, and are con-

sidered a pleasant beverage. One tells them from vinegar by the label.

MARK TWAIN, *A TRAMP ABROAD*, 1880

WINE *n.* Fermented grape-juice known to the Women's Christian Union as 'liquor,' sometimes as 'rum.' Wine, madame, is God's next best gift to man.

AMBROSE BIERCE, *THE DEVIL'S DICTIONARY*, 1911

And Noah he often said to his wife when he sat down to dine,
'I don't care where the water goes if it doesn't get into the wine.'

G. K. CHESTERTON, *WINE AND WATER*

I can find in no book an answer to the question 'How much wine does the average man require?' – a question of great importance. A bottle of Claret among six people is merely tantalising, a bottle each is a little over-generous for a mixed party.

Perhaps as a rough guide the following will serve: a quarter of a bottle – reticence; a half – sufficience; three-quarters – eloquence; and a whole bottle – benevolence.

EDWARD A. BUNYARD, *THE ANATOMY OF DESSERT*, 1929

Religions change; beer and wine remain.

HERVEY ALLEN, *ANTHONY ADVERSE*, 1933

One day in the winter of 1915… I was serving with the Grenadier Guards in front of Laventie. Our Colonel, then the well-known 'Ma' Jeffreys, a super-martinet, and a splendid officer utterly unaffected by sixteen months of the brunt, deprecated the use of alcohol (apart from the regular rum ration) on duty, even under the shocking winter weather and in the front line. It was his wish, although not his actual order, that it should not be taken into the trenches. In a dark and dripping dug-out a bottle of port was being consumed, when the cry 'Commanding Officer' was heard and Colonel Jeffreys began to descend the steps. A young

221

officer in whom there evidently lay the germs of military genius instinctively stuck the guttering candle which lighted the dug-out into the mouth of the bottle. Such candlesticks were common. Everything passed off perfectly. However, six months later this young officer found himself on leave in the Guards' Club, and there met Colonel Jeffreys. 'Have a glass of port wine?' said the Colonel. The subaltern accepted. The bottle was brought and the glasses emptied. 'Does it taste of candle grease?' said the Colonel; and they both laughed together.

WINSTON CHURCHILL, *MY EARLY LIFE (1874–1908)*, 1930

I came upon no wine
So wonderful as thirst

EDNA ST VINCENT MILLAY, *FEAST*, 1934

A good general rule is to state that the bouquet is better than the taste, and vice versa.

STEPHEN POTTER, *ONE-UPMANSHIP*, 1952

In the order named, these are the hardest to control: Wine, Women, and Song.

FRANKLIN PIERCE ADAMS, 1881–1960

ACKNOWLEDGEMENTS

Pavilion Books would like to thank the following for permssion to reproduce copyright material. Every effort has been made to trace and contact all copyright holders but we apologise for any errors or omissions and, if informed, would be glad to make corrections in future editions.

© 1993 Extracted from *Some Other Rainbow* by John McCarthy and Jill Morrell, published by Bantam Press. All rights reserved; extracts from *Dancing in the moonlight* by Ronnie Barker published by Hodder Headline; 'Try Locust When it Comes to the Crunch' by Andrew Morgan (20/11/94) published with the permission of the *Observer*; extract from 'On Food' by Hilaire Belloc reprinted by permission of the Peters Fraser & Dunlop Group Ltd; extract from *Just in Case* by Charlotte Mitchell published by Souvenir Press and reproduced by permission; extract from *The Good Life* © John Esmonde & Bob Larbey, 1976; 'English Girl' by John Agard from *Mangoes and Bullets* published by Pluto Press; extract from 'I Wouldn't Have Missed It' by Ogden Nash from *The Best of Ogden Nash* published by Andre Deutsch Ltd; 'Not That It Matters' copyright A.A. Milne 1919. Reproduced by permission of Curtis Brown, London; extract from *In Defense of English Cooking* by George Orwell copyright © the estate of the late Sonia Brownell Orwell and Martin Secker and Warburg Ltd; 'Greedy Guts' from *Hot Dog and Other Poems* by Kit Wright published by Penguin Books and reproduced with permission; 'Autumn Harvest' by Tim Gilbert published by Macmillan and reproduced with permission; extract